AF600268

Unruly Catholic Feminists

Unruly Catholic Feminists

Prose, Poetry, and the Future of the Faith

Edited by

Jeana DelRosso, Leigh Eicke, and Ana Kothe

State University of New York Press
Albany, New York

Cover art from Shutterstock.com

Published by State University of New York Press, Albany

Printed in the United States of America

Excelsior Editions is an imprint of State University of New York Press

For information, contact State University of New York Press, Albany, NY
www.sunypress.edu

Library of Congress Cataloging-in-Publication Data

Names: DelRosso, Jeana, editor. | Eicke, Leigh, editor. | Kothe, Ana, editor.
Title: Unruly Catholic feminists : prose, poetry, and the future of the faith / Jeana DelRosso, Leigh Eicke, Ana Kothe, editors.
Description: Albany : State University of New York Press, [2021] | Includes bibliographical references and index.
Identifiers: ISBN 9781438485010 (hardcover : alk. paper) | ISBN 9781438485027 (ebook)
Further information is available at the Library of Congress.

10 9 8 7 6 5 4 3 2 1

For the Church Daughters—
May they be our Future Leaders

Contents

Part Three: Spiritual Activism and Utopian Vision

Acknowledgments and Permissions

The editors would like to thank the following individuals and presses for allowing us to republish the pieces we have included in this volume:

"Mystic Trinities" by Kelly Hedglin Bowen was originally published in the spring 2018 edition of *Creative Nonfiction*, issue 66: "Dangerous Creations."

"The Heretic" by C. R. Resetarits was originally published in the Spring 2017 issue of *Interdisciplinary Humanities,* issue 34, no. 1: "Humanities and Religion" as well as her own collection *BROOD* (Mongrel Empire Press, 2015).

"The Lydian Woman Speaks to the Dead Saint" by Becky Gould Gibson first appeared in her book *Indelible,* published in 2018 by The Broadkill River Press.

I shall set up housekeeping with some of my sisters. We shall be unruly women, with no master.

—Hilary Mantel, *The Mirror and the Light*

Introduction

Living with the Past, Envisioning the Future

Countless women around the world find ourselves rooted in Catholic traditions while simultaneously yearning for a church that will grow with us and become something better than—and for—us. Despite our love for the richness of the Catholic culture, many of us cannot forgive the church's continual and persistent failure of so many of its constituents, particularly women. The #MeToo movement has inspired many women to share stories in protest against sexual assault, and it has motivated Roman Catholic women to speak out, too. Anyone who has seen the Netflix series *The Watchers*, which shows women active in researching and revealing the truth about such issues, would be hard pressed to keep their faith in the Catholic Church and its clergy, who undertake, participate in, and cover up the sexual abuse of young girls and boys by Catholic priests.

Pope Francis has made some movement toward progress in the church by advocating for the poor and supporting environmental conservation, and he has even made overtures toward women by commissioning two consecutive studies regarding the possibility of the diaconate for lay women and women religious (for which there is historical precedent in the early but not the modern church, and for which there is long-time precedent in other Christian faiths). Furthermore, as contributor Celia Wexler points out in her recent article in *NBC News*'s "Think," "Pope Frances named the first woman to a managerial position in the Vatican's most important office, the Secretariat of State."[1] He has also loosened the communion restrictions on divorced and remarried Catholics.

Yet his reforms have been limited at best. For one, he has only just begun to support the victims of clergy sexual abuse. While Francis in 2014 appointed a commission for the protection of minors, it wasn't until August 2018 that Pope Francis released a letter, acknowledging the failures of the church: "We did not act in a timely manner, realizing the magnitude and the gravity of the damage done to so many lives. We showed no care for the little ones."[2] And Francis has been particularly disappointing to women's groups seeking equality in the church hierarchy. As Wexler further points out, the first woman in the Secretariat did not replace a man but rather was offered a new title for continuing to do work she was already doing. And as of this writing, no progress has been made on women's ordination to the deaconate, and the ordination of women to the priesthood remains a non-starter. Moreover, calling women theologians "the strawberry on the cake" of the Catholic Church can hardly be viewed as anything other than the Pope patronizing women.[3]

We thus want to explore the future of women in the Catholic Church—a future that, we hope, will go beyond serving as a pretty dessert topping and, instead, actively include the work and aspirations of real women. In our three previous volumes in our Unruly Women Writers series, we attempted to demonstrate the ways in which women engage with the Roman Catholic Church in their writings and in their daily lives. Our first anthology, *The Catholic Church and Unruly Women Writers: Critical Essays* (Palgrave Macmillan 2007), examined both canonical and noncanonical literature, across history and geography, exploring how women writers have been responding to, rebelling against, and reclaiming elements of the Catholic Church from medieval times to the present. Our second collection, *Unruly Catholic Women Writers: Creative Responses to Catholicism* (SUNY Press 2013), offered creative pieces—short stories, poems, personal essays, drama—on this same topic of unruly Catholic women to demonstrate how women express their varying and often-changing relationships with the Catholic Church. Our third volume, *Unruly Catholic Nuns: Sisters' Stories* (SUNY Press

2017), focused specifically on the stories of women religious, current and former, and the ways in which they have spent their lives in struggle with and for the institutional church.

Moving from past to present to future, our newest anthology examines the possibilities and potentials of the roles, responsibilities, and regulations of women in the church, as third- and fourth-wave feminists write about and examine the issues, reforms, progress, and development of new spiritual activism. Here we explore how women are coming to terms with their feminism and Catholicism in the twenty-first century, and we include as well the voices of those who have left the Roman Catholic Church, examining their reasons and their alternative pursuits. Our volume embodies a spiritually, morally, and ethnically diverse group of writers, some of whom have Latinx and indigenous roots, to reflect the changing populations of Catholic congregants and the ways in which the church continues to spread its roots throughout the diaspora.

In the introduction to her recent book *Catholic Women Confront Their Church*,[4] Celia Wexler outlines some of these trends: primacy of conscience, importance of social justice, rejection of the church's opposition to women priests, doubt that ordination is enough, appreciation of Pope Francis but skepticism about what he can do, and faith that transcends the institutional church. Our collection addresses similar issues but focuses more on self-identified third- and fourth-wave feminists, with an eye to the future of the Catholic Church. While fourth-wave feminism is still a work in progress, there has been much critical literature on third-wave feminism. In defining our collection, we rely on R. Claire Snyder's definitive essay, "What is Third Wave Feminism?," which delicately works through the third wave's intimate connection with trends already present in second-wave feminism, its problematic yet liberating use of postmodern antifoundationalist discourses, and its utopian strivings for a better future.[5] Snyder also calls attention to the third wave as "feminism without exclusion," noting that "third-wave feminism necessarily embraces a philosophy of nonjudgment."[6]

Such issues remain active in the fourth wave as well, but fourth-wave feminism also embraces body positivity, celebrating "empowering representations of bodies of different shapes, sizes, colors, and abilities"; most notably, it is also digitally driven.[7] Critics point out that the fourth wave continues to evolve, and Prudence Chamberlain presents it as an " 'affective temporality,' in which a specific period of time engages with and produces affect that in turn engages with and fuels activism."[8] She also highlights how technology has enabled individual women to work together to call out sexism, and how the speed and rapidity of communication facilitate that activism.[9]

We recognize the limitations of the wave terminology for feminism; we are aware that feminist activism was alive and well between the first and second waves, and we are cognizant of the overlap among the waves: for example, a middle-aged feminist today might be considered a third waver by generation but feel much more inclined toward second-wave feminists, because those were the women who taught and mentored her. Similarly, third- and fourth-wave feminists should not be limited by age group. However, we find the wave distinctions useful for categorization purposes and so employ them here.

Accordingly, we have organized this volume in relation to three areas that evoke the third- and fourth-wave issues raised by our contributors: domestic and global social justice, sexuality and motherhood, and spiritual activism and utopian vision. Many of the works included here feature, of course, more than one of these topics, but our goal is to demonstrate how the pieces work with each other and contribute to a conversation about women's roles in the Roman Catholic Church.

Thus, many of our writers address issues of social justice, which, both domestically and internationally, have become even more applicable within feminism and Roman Catholicism. While social justice has a long tradition in the Catholic Church, the church has prohibited, ignored, or denounced some of the issues most vital to feminists. Reproductive rights remain forbidden, racism and sexism do not inspire the opposition they should, and despite the church's opposition to abortion and alleged commitment to human rights, there are many examples of the church's lack of care and action for people with disabilities. While specific religious orders within the church and individual Roman Catholic leaders work for social justice, the international church has not acted on calls from active feminists to speak out on these issues—and to clean its own house. Teresa Cariño, a Filipina pastoral associate inspired by the election of a Latino Pope, remains disappointed: " 'Catholic youth are leaving the church,' she said, as they have grown disillusioned with the pace of change. 'Why stay when there are so many reasons to leave?' is what she hears from her contemporaries."[10]

Our contributors, then, address intercultural and interdenominational issues, diversity, human rights, reproductive rights, work, pedophilia in priests, progress and backlash, women's rights and whistleblowers, violence, disability rights, Black Lives Matter, Native American rights, and healthcare. Some demonstrate how certain areas of social justice have seen progress, and others show how women have had to work around the church to address their concerns. For example, art and worship related to Our Lady of Guadalupe, who has been reinterpreted and embraced internationally as well as increasingly in the United States, show how feminist women can personally rewrite a story and retain inspirational qualities of their family's faith tradition.[11] However, other women, still deeply attached to tradition, face challenges when specific cases of social justice and religious values and beliefs come into conflict. Such conflicts can lead to exceptionally difficult decisions, and the church's strict adherence to doctrine often leaves little room for the consideration of the individual. An expanded understanding of ethnic and cultural diversity, as well as awareness of the impact on women of decisions made by an all-male clergy, infuses the pieces in this volume. While there are signs of generational divide and growth over time, concern, anger, and challenges remain.

Our second category, sexuality and motherhood, addresses two issues that are not always related but that remain major topics of conversation and contention generally, as well as ones in which contemporary Roman Catholic women have more choices than previous generations. Long-familiar topics such as menstruation and reproductive rights remain in active contention, as do questions about interfaith and same-sex marriages. As these issues have developed over time, many have come to the forefront of the conversation, such as the open, public discussion about the anger that stems from clergy abuse and its cover-up. There are movements within the church to confront pedophilia by priests, as in the development of #CatholicToo, inspired by #MeToo and established by liberal feminist religious organizations.[12]

Positive images arise in these conversations as well, such as the individuals and organizations within the U.S. church exploring and tackling issues that the international Roman Catholic Church avoids. One inspiring national story by an ordained deacon demonstrates the learning, development, and acceptance within his community of a child who came out as transgender.[13] Inspired by feminist theology and feminism more generally, our writers also present Jesus as female or God as mother, redefining gender and gendered language. These stories give us hope during bleak political times and religious crises, and we are grateful to our contributors' various and often positive perspectives.

These active revisions of gender also insist upon spiritual activism and lead many of our writers to envision potential utopias. Memories of the waves of radical rethinking of church practices inspired by the Second Vatican Council—including the adoption of vernacular languages, the emergence of women religious from the habit and movement out into the world, and the welcoming of diversity into the pews—cannot be erased by the recent revision/re-version of the liturgy back to patriarchal language or by the Vatican's attack on American nuns. Such attempts to control women's language and agency have only increased women's understanding of ritual, incited women to organize, and inspired women to write their own prayers and develop their own worship.

Similarly, many Roman Catholics find ways to retain the family religious traditions that they knew from their childhood but to adapt these traditions to their own adult beliefs. Some have cultural and familial ties to the church and separate themselves from specific points that trouble them. Feminist theologians offer information, interpretation, and answers to some of our burning questions.[14] Some women actively depart from the church, finding another faith tradition or living without active faith; others find ways to peacefully embrace active worship within the church, working with what they have learned; still others create new rites and rituals. Journalist Pythia Peay describes such movements in "Feminism's Fourth Wave": "At gatherings big and small, many are realizing that putting themselves in the service of the world is feminism's next step. Especially at a time when the United States is viewed with increasing distrust by other countries, feminism's shift cultivating a spiritually informed activism may help to repair our diplomatic ties."[15] Perhaps it will also save our future.

Our contributors thus address multiple issues directly related to third- and fourth-wave feminism and continue the conversation women have had in and with the Catholic Church for centuries. In keeping with our first three volumes, the pieces included here cover varied geographic and ethnic points of view as well as showcase a variety of genres and perspectives. We hope that this book, too, will make a significant contribution to both literary and women's studies because it asks women to write about their experiences with Roman Catholicism and their visions for the future, and it offers contemporary women authors the opportunity to express those experiences as they are lived.

We the editors also have our own stories to tell. We have been reading and publishing the stories of other women for years, and we believe it is time to provide our own perspectives as well, even if only briefly. Thus, Jeana writes,

> I recently went to the funeral of the father of an old and dear friend from my hometown. I saw another old friend there—someone with whom I had attended Catholic schools for what, at the time, seemed like our whole lives: from kindergarten through high school. As we sat together during the service in the funeral home, saying the prayers together—the Lord's Prayer, the Hail Mary, the Glory Be—it occurred to me to wonder how many times she and I had sat next to each other reciting our prayers over the years. And while it had been at least thirty years since we had said those—or

> any—prayers together, and almost that long since we had had a conversation of more than a few pleasantries, it nonetheless felt incredibly familiar and comfortable. Like coming home.
>
> This is what the Catholic Church does for so many of us. It ground us in a tradition that never leaves us: despite our wanderings, our detours, or even our outright rejections. It gives us a solid foundation in faith and spirituality, often so absent from the lives of our colleagues, our neighbors, our friends, our children. It bathes us in doctrine and dogma, infusing our minds with the wealth of knowledge, cultural heritage, religious symbolism, and allusions that inform our reading, our writing, and our daily living. It enriches our thinking, feeling, and acting in the world.

Leigh shares,

> As a cradle Episcopalian, I am grateful that my faith tradition has maintained its three-legged stool—scripture, tradition, and reason—and now embraces the Jesus movement: a loving, liberating, and life-giving God. As our society changes and becomes generally more welcoming and inclusive, most of the Episcopal Church does, too. These points became more active to me when I married. When preparing to marry a Roman Catholic, I worked with both churches. My Episcopal priest, married to a Roman Catholic herself, highlighted the shared beliefs and liturgies of the faiths, and my husband's Roman Catholic priest accepted an interfaith wedding. We were grateful that priests of both traditions led the wedding itself.
>
> However, our first Catholic Mass together after our wedding featured a homily that instructed wives to obey their husbands and make caring for their house and their children their focus in life. Meanwhile, my own religious tradition continued to develop feminist theol-

ogy and came to ordain gay priests and bishops and to celebrate same-sex weddings. It also saw issues of social justice and liberation theology, originally rooted in the Roman Catholic tradition, become more and more active. So I continue to embrace my own faith tradition while remaining fascinated by the Roman Catholic Church, particularly its many inspirational nuns and challenging writers and theologians.

Ana remembers,

> My Spanish mother was not granted an annulment from her first husband until 1979, twenty-five years after marrying her second husband, my father. While the most positive way to describe my parents' relationship with the Roman Catholic church might be "semi-practicing," they were emphatic about giving their daughter a thorough Catholic experience in her childhood—at least through First Communion. This included building a strong relationship with my Godmother—my Madrina—my father's first cousin and a former nun who left the convent to teach at a Catholic elementary school in the Baltimore area.
>
> The relationship with my Madrina over the years, until she passed away in 2004, helped me, in turn, to form a complex relationship with the church. The rest of my family had abandoned Madrina when she openly began a relationship with another woman in the 1960s. However, my parents and the church never turned their backs on her, and so I saw her regularly. After her partner left her, and as she grew older and eventually quite frail, the church took her free of cost into a magnificent Senior Care facility north of the city, where I continued to visit her until her passing. Despite Madrina's unconventional lifestyle, she held onto her faith, and the church was there with her—unlike most of her family—until the very end. My Madrina was as

much an inspiration as the unruly nuns I studied academically. Her life enriched my thinking, doing, and feeling in the world.

Reflecting on the future is an active question at this singular moment in the very long history of the Roman Catholic Church. While change might be slow to come, just the promise of progress may provide hope for women struggling with the conflicts between their church and their sense of their own spirituality. We invite the readers to think of your own stories as you read ours and those of our contributors (and perhaps write and share them, too!). The questions we hope to raise and illuminate by this collection will provide a vital corrective to the contemporary understanding of women's relationships to Catholicism. Rather than simply oppressing or containing women, Catholicism, for many women, drives or inspires us to challenge literary, social, political, or religious hierarchies. In a time when questions of gender and sexuality provoke intense debate within Catholicism and other Christian traditions, and when religion is more and more frequently invoked in political rhetoric, it is imperative to publish works that address women's debates and struggles with the church. Along with other Christian traditions, as well as Judaism and Islam, Catholicism continues to exist as a powerful force in women's lives; by examining how women attempt to reconcile our unruliness with our Catholic backgrounds or conversions and our future hopes and dreams, the editors and contributors to this volume will offer new perspectives on gender and religion today.

Notes

1. https://www.nbcnews.com/think/opinion/pope-francis-put-woman-top-vatican-role-it-shows-how-ncna1119661.

2. https://www.vaticannews.va/en/pope/news/2018-08/pope-francis-letter-people-of-god-sexual-abuse.html.

3. Silvia Poggioli, "After Five Years As Pope, Francis' Charismatic Image Has Taken Some Hits," *All Things Considered*, NPR.org, March 12, 2018.

4. Rowman and Littlefield, 2016, 9–10.

5. *Signs* vol. 34, no. 1 (Autumn 2008): 175–96; 193.

6. Ibid., 188.

7. Kristen Sollee, *Bustle*. October 30, 2015, https://www.bustle.com/articles/119524-6-things-to-know-about-4th-wave-feminism; accessed September 12, 2018.

8. Chamberlain, *Gender and Education*, vol. 2, no. 3: 458.

9. Ibid., 462.

10. Peter Feuerherd, "Francis Still Falls Short with Catholic Women, Feminist Scholars Say," *National Catholic Reporter*, April 19, 2018; https://www.ncronline.org/news/people/francis-still-falls-short-catholic-women-feminist-scholars-say; accessed September 18, 2018.

11. María Del Socorro Castañeda-Liles, *Our Lady of Everyday Life: La Virgen de Guadalupe and the Catholic Imagination of Mexican Women in America*. Oxford Scholarship Online, March 2018.

12. Kate McElwee, "#CatholicToo Organizations Condemn Recent Wave of Clergy Abuse Allegations, Thank Women Religious and Other Survivors For Coming Forward," *Women's Ordination Conference*, August 2, 2018; https://www.womensordination.org/2018/08/02/catholictoo-organizations-condemn-recent-wave-of-clergy-abuse-allegations-thank-women-religious-and-other-survivors-for-coming-forward/; accessed September 18, 2018.

13. Deacon Ray Dever, "Transgender and Catholic: A Parent's Perspective," *U.S. Catholic*, June 2018, https://www.uscatholic.org/articles/201805/transgender-and-catholic-31392; accessed September 18, 2018.

14. In addition to extensive feminist theology, Elizabeth A. Johnson's most recent book includes a conversation between a teacher and student: *Creation and the Cross: The Mercy of God for a Planet in Peril* (New York: Orbis Books, 2018).

15. Pythia Peay, "Feminism's Fourth Wave," *Utne Reader*, March/April 2005; accessed September 18, 2018.

Part One

Domestic and Global Social Justice

Mary

Elizabeth Brulé Farrell

Dusty wooden statue of Mary,
Virgin of Guadalupe, cobwebs hang
from your rays of light.

Your shadow against the wall
at the top of the stairwell
has caught my attention.

I stop and sit with you a while,
another woman who worries
and loves her son as I do.

Both of us illuminated
in front of the window, I offer
my shirttail to wipe both our faces.

You Don't Belong Here

Lauren Frances Guerra

In typical Catholic fashion, my family's church attendance has waxed and waned over the years. Our local Catholic parish, located in a diverse neighborhood in Los Angeles, California, served as a space for celebrating holy days of obligation in community. I was raised as a Roman Catholic and yet my faith journey has not been without its struggle. For a long time, I was uncertain if the religious tradition that I was raised in was what I truly believed and wanted to continue to be a part of. Another important factor in my faith journey is that I didn't realize that the religious practices that my family engages in are what U.S. Latinx theologians describe as Popular Catholicism. Indeed, Latinx religious expression is incredibly complicated and multifaceted, and many of us continue to navigate a space between multiple spiritual traditions.

For many Latinx Roman Catholics, there is often no conflict in attending church on Sunday and participating in another spiritual tradition simultaneously. Allow me to explain how this might function concretely. My maternal grandmother has a small altar in her home. Her altar consists of a few candles, rosary, two large *santos* or statuettes of Mary and Joseph, and a ceramic hand-crafted Niño Jesus. I did not know until quite recently that my grandmother brought all three with her on the long journey when she immigrated from Guatemala City to Los Angeles. The holy family was and continues to be a consistent presence in her home. But in addition to Roman Catholicism, my family also practices elements of *Curanderismo.* This involves spiritual practices such as *limpias* to combat *mal de ojo,* going to *botanicas* on occasion, and consulting *curandero/as.* Both my maternal and paternal grandmothers hold a very special place in their heart for the astrology of Walter Mercado. Yes, Walter Mercado, in his dazzling, sequin glory is a significant spiritual leader for many Latinx people. His astrological segment, which, when I was growing up, would come on during the Spanish broadcast of the evening news, was vital. His predictions and forecast of what was to come served as an important source of knowledge. I distinctly remember that once Walter appeared on screen, the living room was completely captivated by the wisdom he had to offer. And while one might get the impression that looking to astrology or alternative healing practices is something that only the elders of a community engage in, this is not the case. I would like to note that several of my Latinx students (who are part of the millennial generation such as myself) are also devotees of Walter Mercado. They too participate in various Indigenous spiritual practices such as healing circles and sweat lodge ceremonies, to name a few. While more folks seem to be self-identifying as "spiritual not religious," I wonder how many of those folks are actually returning to a more ancient Indigenous or African-based spiritual practice as a way of decolonizing. The syncretic nature of Latinx belief cannot be understated, and I would be remiss not to mention it as part of my own self-reflection in conversation with Roman Catholicism.

Childhood is a formative time for everyone, and our experiences with the church in particular shape us. A few blocks walking distance from my parents' home was a local Catholic parish. It was in a convenient location and thus functioned as our go-to neighborhood church. On one occasion, during a particularly difficult time in our family life, my mother sought the pastoral council of our parish priest. I was about seven years old, and I remember this moment as if it were yesterday. One Sunday, after Mass was finished, my mother and I walked up to the presider so that she could speak with him. He indicated that she should wait for him outside of the sacristy and that he would meet her there shortly. We followed his instructions and waited for him by the sacristy. A few moments later, he appeared and opened the door to the sacristy. He asked my mom to step inside, but I was not received with the same welcome. Instead, he pushed me away and scolded me, saying, "You don't belong here." Before I knew what had happened, the sacristy door was slammed right in my face. In shock, I sat down on the steps of the sacristy in tears to wait for my mom. While my mom was inside speaking with the priest for what may have been only two or three minutes, it felt like an eternity to a young child. While this moment may seem inconsequential to some, it was formative for me.

I asked myself: Why didn't I belong? I thought God loved everyone and that the church itself was supposed to reflect that love. Why wasn't I welcome there? Why didn't I belong? Was it because I was a child? Was it because I was a girl? Was it because I was Latina? That moment marked my relationship with the Roman Catholic Church for a long time. As a child, I also never understood why my church did not have female priests or why women were treated as second-class citizens in general. As I got older, I began to see issues of racism and sexism in the church more clearly.

Unfortunately, women in the Catholic Church are complicit in this type of discrimination as well. Several years later, after the incident previously mentioned, I returned to the same parish to register for confirmation classes. This ended up being a huge mistake as another unfortunate incident occurred. You may be thinking to yourself, Why on earth would you go back to that parish? I attended this parish for my first communion classes and actually had a wonderful experience. My teacher, a very kind Korean American nun, made the first communion classes a lot of fun. I had sincerely hoped that the same would be true for my confirmation classes, but that was not to be the case.

One sunny Saturday morning while in the midst of running various errands, my mother and I stopped by our local parish. The church was conducting sign-ups for the upcoming round of first communion and confirmation classes. A sign-up table was set up in the church parking lot between the church and the parish elementary school. My mom parked in the parking lot, and I hopped out of the car to go sign up at the registration table for Confirmation I. It was meant to be a quick stop at the church: Go, sign up, and continue about the rest of our day.

A female parent volunteer was running the "Confirmation I" registration table and I walked up to her. I indicated that I would like to register for the upcoming confirmation classes. She began with a series of basic questions such as name, address, phone number, et cetera, which went smoothly. Then she asked me if I owned a Bible because I would need one for the confirmation classes. I said that I wasn't sure if my family had one or not. I admitted that we didn't really read the Bible at home. She looked quite disturbed at my response, as if I had committed a mortal sin. Then, she proceeded to yell at me. She screamed: "What do you mean you don't know if you own a Bible?!? You should be reading it every day. Why haven't they shown you the Bible; it is the Word of God. Your family is going straight to hell." In utter shock, I looked at her in disbelief and walked away. I immediately began crying on my walk back to my mother's car in the parking lot. Running through my head were questions like: What did she mean my family was going to hell? Why did she yell at me for not having a Bible? I arrived back at the car. Seeing that I was visibly upset, my mom asked: "What happened??" and I explained to her what had happened when I tried to sign up for classes. My mom's response was, "Are you serious? I can't believe she said that to you. Forget it, you're not doing confirmation then." And that was the end of that.

I did not take confirmation classes until many, many years later when I was a first-year in college. It was at that point that I had enough insight to understand that while my experiences as a child were violent and cruel, they did not represent the whole of Roman Catholicism. My culture makes it difficult for me to completely disconnect from the faith as the two are so deeply enmeshed. It is all far more complicated than it appears on the surface. To leave the Roman Catholic Church would mean losing a significant piece of my identity and heritage.

More importantly, leaving the Roman Catholic Church would mean they've won. It would mean patriarchy, hierarchy, and misogyny had won. I've decided to stay and fight in the hopes for change. I am forever grateful for the Catholic feminist scholars I have encountered who share in this sentiment. In the end, I was able to receive the sacrament of confirmation in the Roman Catholic Church because my university's campus ministry office offered these classes for students. Looking back, this process was incredibly eye-opening for me. I was finally able to choose Catholicism for myself and reconcile my relationship with the church. It was no longer the faith of my parents. As a college student, I was able to exert my own sense of moral agency. In addition, I decided to further explore the tradition even more deeply and become a Theological Studies major. My professors at the time, thankfully, fully supported my inquisitive nature—so much so that it was through their mentoring and support that I decided to pursue a doctorate in Systematic Theology. My female professors (and my female professors of color especially) helped me understand the joy and the struggle of being Roman Catholic.

After years of theological education, I have come to understand how patriarchy and hierarchy function in the church. I am grateful to the fierce feminist theologians who taught me explicitly about feminist discourse. I am grateful to the women (and men) who have taken the Gospel message of infinite love for all people to heart. Most importantly, I have come to realize that the Catholic Church is *exactly* where I belong. This is the incredible power of education and the importance of seeing oneself reflected.

Were it not for being exposed to feminist and U.S. Latinx theologians, I don't know what my relationship with the church would be today. Arguably the most impactful voices have been the voices from within the church. It is far easier to critique from the outside looking in than from the belly of the beast. Collections such as *A Reader in Latina Feminist Theology: Religion and Justice* and *From the Heart of Our People: Latino/a Explorations in Catholic Systematic Theology* have been transformative for me. These books affirmed my own suspicions that being a woman of color in the Roman Catholic Church is very complicated. There are layers and layers of history that need to be unpacked. I firmly believe that it is out of a deep love for the tradition and communities that make up the mosaic of the church that so many of us remain committed to the struggle in the hopes of transformation.

As an educator now myself, I am absolutely committed to breaking down oppressive systems so that no one—regardless of their gender, sexual orientation, or race—will ever be told that they don't belong to the church. I also believe the church does a disservice to those who are struggling with their faith or looking for answers and, instead of being met with welcome, are rebuked. I am committed to create a space for conversation especially for those who self-identify as "nones" or "spiritual not religious" or "agnostic." I refuse to perpetuate a cycle of violence. Simply put, I continue to believe fiercely in a God who is one of radical love and justice. I belong and you belong. We all belong because, at the end of the day, there is infinite space in God's heart for us all.

Salt

Dawn Morais

Hurricanes and earthquakes,
Floods and missiles. Bombs
That shake the bowels
Of the earth. Black lives
Extinguished. White cops
Walk free. We topple
Monuments. We revisit history.

The air is thick with disasters
For post-modern times.
A pitiless torrent
Of pride and punishment.
The kind that turned a woman
Fleeing, into a pillar of salt.

Women have always been salt.
We pickle and preserve.
We keep things from spoiling.
We are vessels for new life.
Our wombs. Our hands.
Our heads and our hearts.
We bear what no man can.

Life's too short for the Summa
Theologica. Aquinas turned
The mystical into the mundane.
His God is not my god.
His angels are not my angels.
All that mansplaining. Enough.
But two hundred years later,
A new plague: The Doctrine
Of Discovery.

Native people needed
Discovery no more than
Women did. They were there.
Till they were erased,
Their labor stolen, their lives
Shelved. Their persons,
Land and rights pulverized
By the raging hooves
Of a Papal Bull.

Women can't wait. The word
Is in our wombs. And the world
Is in our hearts. We ponder
The imponderable. We're done
With being silent.
We have no time for Canon
Law and Papal Dispensations.
Annulments, exorcisms,
Inquiries and investigations.
It's all just bull.

Mostly, we take the Church
By its horns and wrestle it
To the ground without
Saying a word. We believe
In grace. And guts. And truth.

When marriages die
We choose divorce, not
Annulment. Our children
Weren't virgin births.
We will not disavow what
Was. But we will move on.
We will not buy
Permission to be free.
Women say Yes to the pill.
And Yes to the Eucharist.
We do not confess
To a man behind a screen.
The God women speak to
Listens. She understands
When they scream
Inside. How many times
Have we been burned?
It's personal. We've learned:
Don't ask a man with a collar
To wash our sins clean
With one Our Father
And three Hail Marys.

Women have always been salt.
We pickle and preserve.
We keep the Body whole.
We are vessels for new life.
Our wombs. Our hands.
Our heads and our hearts.
We bear what no man can.

We are the church.
Our home is our cathedral,
We evangelize every day
That we pray with our children.
Our welcome is personal.
We nurture all, straight or gay,

We put food on the table,
And take care of grandma.

We cajole and we storm,
We raise hell to protect
The life we bring into the world.
With our wombs. With our hands.
With our heads and our hearts,
We do what no man can.

We are the church.
We evangelize every day
We are in the public square.
We are warriors wiping away
Old wrongs. Warriors
For healthcare and schools.
For water we can drink,
And food we can eat
Without fear.

We are the church.
Discovered or not.
Recognized or not.
Ordained or not.
For without us
There are no priests
No bishops, no cardinals
No pope. No people
In the pews.
Women birth the Word.
As it was in the beginning,
Is now, and ever shall be
World without end
Amen.

Citizen Voices

Jennifer Hall Lee

There is a photograph of a woman standing alone in front of a church. She wears a white dress and looks directly at the camera. She holds a purse down at her side. Oddly, the woman stands next to a brown ladder that extends from the ground and up out of the frame. I don't know why the picture taker chose to position the woman next to the ladder. The image is compelling because the ladder is in the center and the woman is to the side. The picture is mine and the woman is my great grandmother.

I have another photograph that shows a woman standing with a young girl, also in front of a church. The girl wears a white communion dress and the woman wears a hat. There is a sign on the brick wall behind them that tells me this snapshot was taken at Holy Family Church. The woman is my grandmother, the girl is me, and the church is on Staten Island, one of the five boroughs of New York City.

Historically, Staten Island was known for its numerous waterways, and as a girl I played in a small brook near my home, but the brook was paved decades ago to make way for new housing developments that have dominated the island.

One would never know that fresh and saltwater streams were a vital part of Staten Island. One of those brooks was named Willow Brook, but it too is gone.

Photos provide a visual history of people's lives, and these particular photos of mine reveal a relationship between the Catholic religion and the women in my family. Images tell stories, we all know that, but the absence of images tells stories, too.

There is no photo of my mother alone in front of a church. Nor is there one of my daughter and me at Holy Family Church. But I, too, have a relationship with the Catholic Church.

In my bedroom I have a ceramic figurine of the Virgin Mary. Her head is bowed passively, and her hands are in prayer. This pastel-colored icon has been in my family since I was born. It once stood on my mother's dresser, and now it stands on mine. At some point in its journey it was defaced, by me.

At the age of eight I drew a vertical line on Mary's gown with a ballpoint pen. If my mother noticed she never said anything. Over the years, through multiple moves, the icon was packed away and stayed in a box until she gave it to me when I was an adult.

The Blessed Virgin Mary can be a powerful figure, but in the male ethos of the Church, her effectiveness is muted and constrained. I often wonder when women will take their rightful place in the Church hierarchy.

My mother, grandmother, and I all rebelled against the Catholic Church.

One of our first acts of rebellion occurred when my grandmother was a teenager and she and her brother went to their priest because their mother, my great grandmother, was being beaten by their father, who was an alcoholic. The priest denied them help and said they had to respect their father. My grandmother was incensed.

Later another act of rebellion happened when my mother was walking to her Catholic school with her sister and she announced that she did not believe in God. My aunt was thunderstruck. How could someone even entertain that thought?

The earth is round and not flat. One person who voices a dissenting viewpoint can change the world.

Although my aunt certainly believed in God and science as a young girl, my mother's words were new to her.

Several years after that day my grandmother gave birth to her fifth child, a boy with Down syndrome. He is my uncle.

My favorite picture of my grandmother, my uncle, and me is a simple black-and-white square image. It is 1966, and my ten-year-old uncle is wearing a baseball cap, and on top of my head is my Easter bonnet. My grandmother is smiling and there are daffodils growing in the yard.

Daffodils are one of the ubiquitous flowers of Staten Island.

After the birth of my uncle in the 1950s, our family doctor told my grandparents that since my uncle had Down syndrome they should send him to live in an institution. The one he was referring to was on Staten Island, and it was called Willowbrook State School.

My grandfather drove to see Willowbrook for himself, and I don't know if he went inside, but when he came home he said to my grandmother that they couldn't send their son to live there. My uncle was raised at home.

Willowbrook was an institution for mentally retarded people (that was the term used in those days), and it was a sprawling complex of many late 1930s brick buildings on hundreds of acres of land. It was one of the largest employers on Staten Island.

By the time my uncle was born it was populated with residents from in and around New York City. Not all were mentally handicapped as some had physical disabilities.

As my uncle grew, my grandmother devoted herself to his life and education.

She was an active parent in Staten Island AID, a nonprofit organization for people with mental disabilities. I accompanied my grandmother there often, and I sometimes went bowling with my uncle and the people in his program.

It was also during this time that my mother worked as a social worker at Willowbrook State School.

Willowbrook. For me the word doesn't mean a meandering bountiful waterway filled with fish. For me it has the stigma of scandal.

This institution dominated our lives for several years. It no longer exists—partly because of my mother's activism combined with the parents of the residents who fought for better conditions.

Life at Willowbrook was horrific. There is no other way to say this. In the early seventies there were six thousand people living there, and the conditions were inhumane.

In 1971 my mother, another social worker, and a doctor blew the whistle on the administration at Willowbrook.

Whistleblowers. We all love heroes, and many people like to see themselves as a person who will heroically stand up and be the lone voice for justice. It sounds romantic and exciting, but being the person who tells on someone can be lonely and, in the face of adversity, it's much harder than it seems.

How can it be hard to tell the truth or point out inhumanity? Societies are complex groups and patterns of human behavior are hard to break. Whistleblowers demand you look and see something you have avoided seeing.

For example, the whistleblowers for Willowbrook approached several well-known progressive organizations who fought consistently for people's legal rights and asked for help in getting attention for the human rights violations at Willowbrook. Residents were abused and barely had clothes. Food and medical care was inadequate.

These well-meaning people listened to the whistleblowers with sympathy, yet couldn't help because there were other things commanding their attention. My mother, the social worker, and the doctor had to find a way to shake loose the old way of thinking that enabled people to see disabled people as outcasts or "others." How could that change when the entire society, for the most part, had always thought that way?

As each organization declined their assistance the whistleblowers persisted, and finally a young female reporter, Jane Kurtin, at the *Staten Island Advance*, the local paper, acted and wrote an article detailing the abuses of the people at Willowbrook. One of her articles was called "Willowbrook: Inside the Cages." The journalist told the truth.

My mother didn't think the newspaper would publish it, but they did.

This initial article fueled a firestorm of outrage that reached state politicians. I can only imagine how it must have felt for

Staten Islanders to wake up to their morning paper and read the first words about exposing the illegalities at Willowbrook. Many would have known someone who worked there; perhaps they themselves were employees.

The article blew the secret out of the darkness. I sometimes think that, when many people see a closeted truth for the first time, the conversation shifts and new words come forth. In the face of a brave voice of dissent, old sayings or talking points are set aside because they no longer serve an outdated need, which was to keep a truth hidden. Sayings such as "It's always been that way" no longer work.

In the middle of this omnipresent turmoil my mother took me inside one of the wards at Willowbrook. It was called Ward 6.

I was nine years old and she held my hand and we walked through a large hallway into a big open room. I think the walls were green, but I don't know for sure. I remember I was nervous. Inhuman sounds were bouncing off walls and, as we approached a doorway, I could see where the sounds were coming from.

My brain catalogued this moment.

The ward smelled like the Staten Island Zoo. The sounds were guttural and unexpected. There were no perceivable conversations, just shouts and echoes. The smell was primal and human. I wanted to leave, but I couldn't.

There were long lines of benches, and this is where people sat together and alone. Many might have had Down syndrome but I don't know for certain. Some people rocked back and forth. I don't remember what they were wearing. There was no organization to this room, just people without real furniture. I heard the lonely echoes of people using their voices, but with no one to touch them.

I waited and observed while my mother talked to people in the room.

Being in a ward at Willowbrook was a difficult experience, and the wards were a point of contention for the parents who were protesting for better conditions. The wards were always locked. When a parent came to visit, their child was always dressed and brought out to the parent. For a parent to enter a ward unannounced was not an option. Open wards was one of their demands.

During the height of the tensions the anger of parents spilled over, and the administration was having trouble containing blowback. Media coverage was never ending. The director of Willowbrook practically blew a gasket, and one day in a terrible fury, he ordered the wards opened.

The doors were unlocked and the parents flooded in.

One mother saw her son and screamed his name: "Mikey, my Mikey, is sitting next to someone eating his own shit!"

She went hysterical.

During those Willowbrook years my grandmother supported my mother every step of the way. My grandmother had no fear about picking up a telephone and calling someone to discuss an important problem. She called the chaplain who worked at Willowbrook to talk with him about the conditions. The chaplain did nothing.

This is where Willowbrook and Holy Family Church come together for me.

My mother and the doctor were fired from their jobs because they broke the rules. They were not supposed to meet with the parents agitating for changes. And, of course, by going to the newspaper they opened the doors for the world to see what was inside that institution.

Now without a job, my mother moved us in with my grandmother, grandfather, and my uncle.

Willowbrook had become a national scandal. Changes at Willowbrook were being discussed.

My grandmother started to work for the rights of "mentally retarded citizens." Those were her words.

As I look back I see that by referring to disabled people as citizens she was changing the mindset of those to whom she was speaking. How can one deny rights to citizens?

As our country was de-institutionalizing, the next logical step was to create housing for people with disabilities. My grandmother and other parents wanted to start a group home in our neighborhood.

There was a town hall meeting at Holy Family Church. The town hall was a disaster. I didn't attend, but my grandmother told me about it afterward while sitting at her kitchen table. She had stopped reading her newspaper and lowered her voice and said, "I couldn't believe the things I heard people say." She said it was "shocking." She never told me exactly what they said because she didn't want to repeat it, but what she witnessed in her church hurt her deeply. These were people in her community speaking in a house of God as to why they did not want a group home in the neighborhood. I am sure that horrible names were used and fears of criminality were voiced. Maybe people worried about property values.

Beyond the hate coming from some Staten Island residents, it was the void created by the priest himself that cut her even deeper.

He didn't speak up. My grandmother said to me, "He just sat there in silence. He never said a word."

His reluctance to assert his moral authority in his church was more than she could take. She wrote him a letter.

There is no copy of that letter, but I do know that she told him that he had a duty to speak up to the cruel words of those community members. He was the priest, after all. She wrote that she would no longer attend Holy Family Church.

Well, this made him speak up. He called her on the telephone. I laugh now as I visualize him calling her number on a rotary phone because her number had a prefix, SA-7, or Saint George Seven.

Over the phone she read him the riot act. I don't know how he replied, but I remember her saying that the priest really didn't have much to say so she hung up.

As she spoke to me her voice was strong, and she wielded an immense amount of moral authority.

My grandmother and Holy Family Church were finished.

In life there is always the opportunity to make the right choice in any situation, and in that town hall the priest failed a fundamental test of Christianity. He didn't speak up for those who cannot speak for themselves.

She never returned, nor did she ever attend another church. But she never lost her faith.

When I lived with her, and after that when I stayed with her during vacations, I often accidentally walked in on her as she knelt by her bed and prayed. I could hear her whispered words and I carefully walked out of the room to leave her in peace.

As the years went on my grandmother had a public presence, and she gave speeches as she fought for the rights of mentally disabled citizens. She was well respected.

I considered myself a radical feminist.

On a holiday break from college I was in my grandmother's kitchen and as she was making herself a cup of tea, I asked her if she believed in abortion. This was a question for which I knew the answer (my grandmother had been Catholic all her life and didn't believe in abortion), but after all these years I wanted to hear how she had changed. She said that after her experiences of being a parent of a Down syndrome child and having seen how people treat people with disabilities she has changed her mind on the topic of abortion.

Her words had weight because they expressed real change that occurred over time.

Later, when my uncle was an adult she pinned small metal icons of saints on my uncle's shirts and sweaters. Sometimes there were several on one safety pin. One was usually the Infant of Prague, her mother's favorite image.

I have two of these medals on their original safety pin in my jewelry box.

Willowbrook was officially closed in 1987, now a symbol of essentially a medieval past.

I will never underestimate the power of persistence and the written word.

When my grandfather died, a very young priest gave the Mass. I sat next to my mother, and we listened. The priest's words had no meaning for me. At one point he said that my grandfather had sins. I felt my mother move and stiffen. As the priest asked us to repeatedly stand and sit and stand and sit, my mother sat the entire time.

Later, as we left the cemetery she said to me that his words bothered her because my grandfather had raised a Down syndrome child. What *sins* could this young priest possibly be talking about? What did this priest know about my grandfather's experience?

Indeed, why was he given moral authority to cast judgment on a man who spent his life raising my uncle with love? It was my grandfather who made the decision that my uncle would not live in Willowbrook.

My grandparents had more moral authority than this priest.

Later in my life I adopted a girl who had been in an orphanage. I named her after my grandmother because I wanted her to know she was part of a family that fought for the right things, and for my grandmother this came at a cost; she ended her relationship with the Catholic Church.

I don't believe that religion solely lies in any church; that's far too narrow a belief. And I certainly don't believe that only men can be priests.

The Church keeps priests male in order to hold onto male power. Symbolically, it sets up a system of power in which women are perceived as less than men.

When a female journalist recently asked Pope Francis his opinion on the possibility of women becoming priests, he rejected it, citing that priests essentially act as stand-ins for Christ and therefore must be male. This is laughable.

But what was more interesting to me was her response to him. The journalist asked, "Never?" I heard it as plaintive and desirous of a different answer. In my opinion her question was asked within a mindset that we needed men's permission. That is not how change happens.

By keeping priests male, the Church maintains patriarchal dominance of women and children, which reinforces the myth that men have authority as the ultimate narrators.

The image of a woman as the ultimate voice of authority in the Church can help change the world.

The closure of Willowbrook in 1987 was the result of people standing up to power. There was a time when its power seemed impenetrable. But in reality Willowbrook could and would be closed, and it would take all the existing institutions with it.

When women demand that they can serve as voices for Christ, then the Pope will have no choice but to stand back and allow women to take their rightful place in the Catholic Church.

Inundated

Dinorah Cortés-Vélez

The horizontal poem that follows depicts the quasi-erotic attachment to knowledge that Mexican nun Sor Juana Inés de la Cruz (1648 or 1651–1695) displayed in nearly everything she wrote. In the poem, she is portrayed in a state of "metaphysical inundation," in Gerard Flynn's apt phrase. "Inundated" muses over what she would tell Knowledge should she be able to write it a love letter. This relates to current feminism today as much as ever, as it shows the investment of libidinal energy into the acquisition of knowledge. These images of sex-positivity may seem paradoxical when referring to a cloistered nun, but they ultimately highlight that the activity of the mind is libidinal and subliminal in nature. One may also say there is queerness in the obsessive and lovelorn characteristics of the letter. Sor Juana embraces queerness in her portrayal of gender-related issues throughout her vast literary output. For example, she claims in one of her poems that her body is neuter, that it doesn't have a sex. She reveals a willingness to question. As a defender of women's rights and protofeminist, Sor Juana asserts that knowledge is not exclusively the province of maleness. This poem-letter celebrates that sentiment.

"Inundada"

Poema-carta de Sor Juana a su intelecto:

Me naufragas. Sin tregua, a la deriva va, acantilada de lestrigones, la leve nave de esta gana submarina que inundas en mí, con tu urgencia anochecida de hacerme verlo todo. Tu empeño insaciable es parte de la morfología de mi anhelo, que no se cansa. Se me entraña el sedimento de tanta querencia, dejándome extenuada y dichosamente infeliz. Cada encuentro, tuyo y mío, me deja queriendo dibujar la curvatura de tus pliegues y habitarte hasta donde no dé más, pero ¡cómo perplejas mi habilidad para reinventar la felicidad hasta siempre vernos en cariñosa refriega!

En demudada contienda, me arponeas como a un pez, y yo, me dejo, mientras mis ojos recorren el relieve de tus rutas inusitadas. Me horada entonces la luz lunática de una voluntad, sinuosa como talud, de aprehender, desvariada, ufana y atolondrada, tu vuelo, en el vértigo de nuestro beso. Luego me sobreviene la zozobra y quedo encallada en el costado de nuestro afán compartido. Grano a grano muerdo, de a pocos, el arenisco banco de nuestro vértigo, tálamo de nuestro enamorado denuedo. Mas, aquí me tienes, otra noche más, desapercibidas las defensas, erguido, en su desnudez, el mástil de mi ansia, siempre listo para enarbolar las velas de tu movimiento.

"Inundated"

Poem-letter from Sor Juana to her intellect:

You shipwreck me. Without truce, adrift there it goes, thrown into the abyss of Laestrygonians, the tenuous vessel of this submarine yearning with which you inundate me with your dawning urgency of making me see everything. Your insatiable tenacity is part of the morphology of my longing, which doesn't wear down. The sediment of the fondness gets deep into me, leaving me exhausted and joyously unhappy. Each encounter between you and me ends with me wanting to draw the contours of your folds and inhabit you to the limit, but how you perplex my ability to reinvent happiness until seeing each other forevermore in this loving scuffle!

In a muted contest, you harpoon me like a fish, and I allow it, while my eyes follow the relief of your unusual routes. I am pierced by the lunatic light of a will, sinuous as a continental slope, of apprehending—delirious, jubilant, and bewildered—your flight in the vertigo of our kiss. Then anxiety overcomes me, and I remain run aground by the side of our shared eagerness. One grain at a time, I bite the sandy bank of our vertigo, thalamus of our loving daringness. And here you have me, one more night, my defenses down, erect in its nakedness the mast of my yearning, always ready to raise the sails of your movement.

Note: I'd like to thank Dr. Michael Roeschlein for his help rendering the English version of this poem-letter.

A Person Is a Person

Anonymous

I'm fourteen years old. It's my second week at a private all-girls' Catholic high school in my hometown of Buffalo, N.Y. It feels like I've already been here too long. I can barely keep up with the homework—almost five hours nightly. Unlike my elementary school teachers, these high school ones do not fawn over me or single me out as special. As for the students, they wear brands like Express and J. Crew (because the school was founded by an order of nuns who never wore the habit, we are spared uniforms). I feel out of place in my K-Mart-purchased clothes. Today, over my floral summer dress, I have pinned a button my mother gave me. It shows the image of a developing unborn child—a fetus, as it's officially called—in the womb. Underneath it, in blue letters, appears this phrase: *A person is a person, no matter how small.* I believe in this statement wholeheartedly; I have believed it ever since I learned how babies were made.

Making my way through the cafeteria line, I am served the day's special—chicken souvlaki—and take my seat with the seven girls I've chanced to sit with since the first day. I usually eat in silence, rarely joining their conversations about movies I haven't watched and music I don't listen to. But today, one of them, Debra—a black-clad Goth in fishnets—turns to me. "What's with that button?" she asks.

"It's a pro-life button," I say, caught off guard.

"Well, obviously. But why are you wearing it to school?"

I swallow, wondering if I should ask her the same about the skull necklace she's wearing around her neck. Instead, I decide to keep it simple.

"I believe in the right of an unborn child to live," I say.

In response she rolls her eyes. "Come on. If you got pregnant, what do you think you'd do?"

The question freezes me in mid-bite of chicken souvlaki. *Me? Pregnant?* The absurdity of that idea is laughable. At fourteen I have never kissed a boy and have no interest in doing so. In eighth grade the boys bullied me constantly, so I am looking forward to four years in an all-girls' school as my own version of heaven. My life involves learning Bach's Inventions for my weekly piano lesson and memorizing verbs for the Polish Saturday School I attend. I'm giving serious thought to becoming a nun; I've been told that sex before marriage is immoral and would never even think of doing it. Me? Pregnant? How could this little bitch think something like that about *me*?

However, the question forces me to contemplate the possibility of this scenario, unlikely as it sounds. "Have the baby and raise it," I say, and mean it, even though it still seems as likely as me planning a move to Mars.

~

Twenty years later, some things have changed; others clearly have not. Thus far, I have never been pregnant. I've also not become a nun. While I don't wear a button, I do have a large "Respect Life" magnet on my filing cabinet. And as for Debra, whom I self-righteously dismissed in that cafeteria conversation . . . Our adversarial interactions eventually bloomed into long, reflective discussions; two decades later, she is one of my dearest friends.

While I may not feel I've changed all that much, the world certainly looks quite different than it did in 1998. 9/11, the defining moment of my early adulthood. Two wars. Economic and ecological crises. The election of my country's first nonwhite president. And then, his controversial successor. After languishing in despair for a few days after Donald Trump's inauguration, I decided to focus on the issue closest to my heart: immigration. I work as a Spanish teacher at a liberal arts college in the Midwest. There's a small population of undocumented Spanish-speaking immigrants in my community and not many bilingual interpreters to help them, so I soon find myself accompanying them to legal and medical appointments, driving them to their court dates, and gathering up winter clothes for them. One Monday, at the end of my workday, I receive a call from Yolanda, a nineteen-year-old who came to this country fleeing gang violence in her small town in Honduras. The organization I work with set her up to attend the public school, and I've been spending a day each week helping her with her history homework, swallowing a lump in my throat as I explain the Spanish-American War of 1898 and the age of twentieth-century U.S. imperialism it ushered in, affecting her country and nearly every other one in the Western Hemisphere.

"I need to talk to you now," she says. "Can you come over?"

Twenty minutes later I am seated in her living room. Her cousin Joaquina pours a glass of Coca Cola for me and then sits to join the conversation. They explain hurriedly that Yolanda needs me to drive her to a special clinic in another city, that she is not well, that she needs help. When I try to ask about the nature of her health issue, both of them look at the floor, clearly hesitant to tell me. Closing my eyes briefly for a moment, I decide to fill in the gap.

"Are you pregnant?" I ask.

Solemnly, Yolanda nods. "Yes," she says. There is a pause before she says the words I know are coming. "And I don't want to be."

~

At nineteen, I am still a virgin—by anyone's definition of the term.

I have opted for college, just as I always assumed I would, but in sending out those applications, I passed over Boston College and Loyola and Notre Dame in favor of an ultra-secular liberal arts college just outside New York City. It was a rough transition, going to a place where church attendance seems about as hip and sophisticated as country line dancing. The fact that 9/11 happened during my first week of college didn't make for a smooth start, nor did the fact that I was housed in a triple with two roommates who instantly bonded over their shared love of musical groups like the Smiths—while I was the odd one out.

But now, halfway through my sophomore year, I am seeking to remake myself. I have interned for a Latin American film festival and written for a publication that has allowed me to interview comedian/economist Ben Stein and novelist Jonathan Safran Foer. I have studied anthropology and medieval history and Latin American surrealist literature. I've found a group of friends to explore Manhattan with—we see the musical *Chicago* on Broadway and a Tori Amos concert at Radio City Music Hall and a poetry reading at Cooper Union; we eat in delectable restaurants and shop for discounts in Chinatown. I lead a charmed life.

And yet, like Miriam of Nazareth before she received the news that would change the world, I do not yet know man. It's a reality that my more experienced friends look down on me for, unable to take me seriously when discussing relationships. For while college has changed me in many ways (I no longer believe that being gay is morally wrong; I no longer trust the U.S. government as I did as a child; I now feel obligated to keep up with current events), I still have never had a boyfriend, and I still believe, as I was taught all my life, that all extramarital sex is wrong.

And yet, I would be lying if I said I felt no envy when watching a handholding couple walk across campus, clearly smitten with each other. I fear the potential consequences of getting into that situation, knowing that most young men in this secular world would not want to date a woman who was unwilling to go to bed with them. And I must admit that I am proud of my virginity. All my life, I have been told that the female role models I should follow—Mary, or saints like Therese of Lisieux, or Catherine of Siena, or my own confirmation saint, Dymphna of Geel—were women who had taken vows of chastity. To do anything else, it seemed, would be less morally correct, less pure.

One day, while discussing these views with my friend Rachel—a nondenominational Christian who has had a serious boyfriend since high school and believes firmly in sexual freedom—she looks a little hurt by the views I express. "Do you really think that whether or not a woman has had sex is the measure of her worth?" she asks indignantly. "Do you realize what you are saying about me when you state that belief? Do you understand just how much you are putting me down?"

~

My head spins as Yolanda shares her news. She's asking me to make an appointment, drive her to the clinic, and interpret for her if there are no Spanish-speaking staff on hand. "I'll pay you," she says, and I shake my head. Taking a deep breath, I try to present her with some alternatives. She has given her reasons: that she is not ready to have a child, that she is in too much debt to take on the expense. When she tells me that she does intend to build a future with the baby's father, I mention that there are people in the community who could help her in raising the child. "I could take care of it," I say, in a statement that I know is not completely sincere. She shakes her head. I introduce the possibility of adoption, telling her that this country, this state, this city are filled with people who would love to adopt a child. Again, she shakes her head. "I'm not going to have a baby just to give it away," she says simply.

I tell her that I am not sure if I can accompany her to this appointment—that doing so goes against my religious beliefs. Is there anyone else she might get a ride from? She shakes her head. "No." She has told her mother back in Honduras, as well as her boyfriend here in our town, and of course her cousin Joaquina—but apart from them, she does not want anyone to know. Not her cousins or others in the Central American immigrant community, not any of the local justice advocates who have been helping her. And so I find myself doing something I never thought I would. She gives me the name and number of a clinic two hours away—a clinic she heard about from an old American friend of Joaquina, a woman who lives in another state. Before I can really stop and contemplate what I am doing, I am making the call, setting an appointment in just one week's time. Even though I am still reluctant to commit, I already know that I will be the one to go with her.

~

At twenty-four, I am still a virgin—but only by the definition of the term used in conventional, patriarchal society. By other definitions, including Pope John Paul II's, my virginity might be up for debate. I've finished college and taken a job at a private bilingual international school in Managua, Nicaragua, where I teach English literature and writing to a rather rambunctious group of high school students—sons and daughters of the nation's wealthy elite.

It's a tough job. I'm an inexperienced teacher with no real strategy for handling these young people who are used to being waited on by housekeepers, maids, gardeners, and drivers—and who expect similar treatment from me. It's reached the point where I begin many mornings with a nervous feeling in my stomach, wondering what kind of prank the students are going to pull today—whether turning their desks around when I enter the room or standing up to sing the Nicaraguan National Anthem in protest against a quiz. After the final bell rings, I return exhausted to the home where I am living—a house owned by the school, cared for and watched over by a live-in housekeeper who pours me a cold drink of cacao as consolation, leaving me to feel a certain amount of self-reproach at my constant complaining. My job is not nearly as difficult as hers, and the payment I receive is about ten times more.

Still, it is hard. I decided to teach in Nicaragua because I wanted to gain experience and make a difference. While I am definitely gaining experience, it is clear that I am not going to make any positive difference. This realization is tough for me, as is the growing loneliness I have been starting to feel. Most of the other teachers I work with, while friendly enough, are not eager to become my friends. They have their own lives, their own families, their own groups of friends they like to go out with on weekends.

But one time, on a rare occasion when I do go out salsa dancing at a local club, I meet Eduardo, a construction worker studying computer programming as much as time allows. We dance all night and exchange numbers. One month later, we are seeing each other almost every day. On Friday nights we go out dancing; he comes back and sleeps beside me. Lazy mornings bleed into lackadaisical afternoons; we get up again, go out again, stay together again. On Sunday mornings we go to Mass at a lovely church called San Agustín; we walk around the Huembes market and eat freshly made *gallo pinto* and plantains at a lunch counter; we stop off to visit his mother and sisters—a low-income family living in a modest neighborhood near the market. This becomes our new routine. I can tell that Catalina, my housekeeper, is looking on this disapprovingly; I get the sense that I shouldn't let my work colleagues know that I am dating this young man. Are we serious? Is there a future? Will we end up getting married? Part of me dares to hope so, but another part of me knows that this is just a phase, that a large part of why I am dating him is that I am alone in a foreign country, young, and seeking adventure. And so, as we walk through Managua holding hands, I feel a certain amount of shame. Whatever idea of "innocence," of "virtue" I was holding onto . . . It no longer seems to apply.

~

On the day of Yolanda's appointment, my alarm rings at 5:30. I drag myself out of bed and begin my morning routine—put the kettle on, jump into the shower, scroll through emails. A text message arrives from Joaquina at six a.m.: "Are you coming?" she asks. It's as if both of them are afraid I might bail at the last minute.

But I don't. I make the fifteen-minute drive from my apartment to theirs. I call the attendance office at her school, informing them that she is ill and will not be in today. Then, we are off on the road.

"How are you feeling?" I ask her.

"Fine," she says.

"Yeah?" I ask.

"I mean, I'm a little sad. I do wish I could have had this child. But I'm just not ready," she says.

I think to myself how all of this could have been prevented if she had known the facts about where babies come from. Right after she broke the news about her pregnancy, I did my best to give her a ten-minute sex education talk, letting her know about some of the contraceptive methods available. She replied that she had never heard of them. This does not shock me—after all, before coming to the U.S. she did not go to school past the sixth grade, and if I had not learned about these things in school, I might not have learned from any other source. As in her case, my very conservative mother did not tell me.

We drive into the city. I take her for a required blood test at the hospital, then out for breakfast at a local clinic. I check my watch. Our appointment at the Margaret Fuller Clinic—named for a nineteenth-century women's rights activist, a member of Ralph Waldo Emerson's Transcendentalist circle—is at noon. We make our way back to the car, and I drive toward the address I looked up earlier.

Just as I'm wondering if I'll be able to spot the clinic while driving, I see what is unmistakably it. A group of about five protesters is standing in front, waving signs I can see from the road. "BABIES ARE MURDERED HERE!" screams one of the signs in large letters. "IT'S A CHILD, NOT A CHOICE," asserts another. I gulp, thinking of when I was fourteen and stood with my mother on a busy street in our hometown for the National Life Chain, holding a sign saying, "Abortion Kills Children." I think of all the other times, more recently, when I have stood outside abortion clinics with her, praying the rosary. She and her group have never been antagonistic toward the women seeking the clinic's services, but these protesters—five men, one woman—do not seem nearly so peaceful.

"Who are those people? What are they doing here?" asks Yolanda as we make our way from the car toward the clinic.

"I'll explain later," I say, taking her hand and trying to ignore the knot in my stomach. I look down at the ground, unable to meet their eyes, struggling to ignore the voices—*Hey! Stop and talk to us for a moment. You're not really going in there, are you?*

Moving as quickly as I can, clenching Yolanda's hand more tightly, I throw open the door. Inside, I am amazed to find the environment as politicized as outside. Behind the reception desk, T-shirts hang from the wall. "American conservatism: shrinking government just small enough to fit inside your vagina!" says one. "Wild Woman!" exclaims another. As we step in, the receptionist behind the desk tells us to leave our purses and coats on a rack in the hallway. No bags are allowed inside. I puzzle over this for a moment, only later realizing that the reason for this is because the clinic regularly receives bomb threats.

I help Yolanda to check in, thinking my interpretation services will be needed, but almost immediately a Spanish-speaking staff member is called upon. She asks me to sit down and takes Yolanda under her charge. For the next four hours, my task will only be to wait.

~

At twenty-nine, I'm a graduate student living in Toronto. I have marched on the G20 Summit and protested the former School of the Americas at Fort Benning, a notorious military institution where students were once trained in torture; I volunteer at a mental health hospital and sign petitions to stop deforestation and support native people's rights. My progressive credentials seem solid, if I do say so myself. But I always find myself in a heated discussion when the issue of abortion comes up.

"I believe it's wrong," I tell one friend, a young U.S.-Canadian dual citizen whom I met volunteering for the mental health hospital. "I don't necessarily think it should be illegal."

"So, you mean it's wrong for you?" he asks, hoping that I will give an answer that expresses the nonjudgmental tolerance that is arguably the greatest strength and greatest weakness of my generation.

"No," I say. "I think it's objectively wrong," I say. When an awkward silence ensues, I go on. "But that doesn't mean I can judge the people who do it. After all, war is wrong, and that is not illegal—they tried that, and it didn't work. My cousin is a

West Point graduate fighting in Afghanistan now, and that doesn't make me love him less. I see abortion the same way," I explain.

Another friend seems determined to get me to identify as pro-choice. "You don't think it should be illegal. You think women should choose. That means you're pro-choice," she says.

Logically, it sounds true. But if it is, then this is not a truth I want to accept. Because I still think abortion is wrong. I struggle for words, wishing the argument could be framed in a different way.

~

"Stop! Talk to us!" one of the protesters implores me. I hate going outside, but I have no way to avoid it unless I want to risk getting a ticket due to an expired parking meter.

"Do you really want to be an accomplice in a murder?"

There is part of me that would like to stop and talk to them, that would like to say, *I'm on your side. I like abortion about as much as you do.* I am thinking about how the two sides might have more in common than they admit. While some on the pro-choice side do genuinely believe abortion to be a good thing, there are many who see it as a last resort.

Back in the waiting room, I share my views with another woman waiting her turn to be called. She looks to be in her late thirties, and she is visibly pregnant. A man sits beside her. They have been there a while; I assume they are waiting for someone. Earlier we were making friendly small talk about local restaurants, and she has a nice smile, so I decide to share my feelings about the protesters outside. I mention that I have protested abortion clinics, though never as aggressively as these people are doing. She nods sympathetically. "There may be a space for pro-life pro-choice dialogue, but this is not it."

In the middle of the room, amid a stack of magazines, I notice a book of anonymous essays. I pull it out and begin reading these various accounts of women who have undergone abortion. All of them say they do not regret it—hardly a surprise; those who regret it probably were not selected for inclusion in this volume. Many of them say they initially felt guilt and shame about abortion because they were raised Catholic. From the sound of it, none of them is still practicing.

At that moment, the woman's name is called. "Karen?" I cringe. She is visibly pregnant. Up until now, I did not believe—could not believe—she was here for an abortion. I figured she was here to support someone else, like me, waiting for someone. And she is going to terminate her pregnancy?

Disgusting.

But then, I stop myself. I remind myself that I do not know her reasons for being here. There could be many, including just a check-up. And if it is abortion . . . maybe she has learned that her baby will be stillborn, or likely to die soon after birth. What judgment can I make about her experience? How much can I really claim to know about the life of a stranger?

~

I'm thirty-one. It's summer, and I am visiting my parents on a break from grad school. One morning my mother asks me to go with her, to "stand outside for a while." I know what this means. It's a Tuesday, and every Tuesday at noon, a group of people from Respect Life committees from different parishes gathers to pray the rosary outside one of our city's notorious abortion clinics. I have gone here with her before, though it has been a few years.

"Thank you for coming with me," she says on the drive down. "I know you probably don't want to do this . . ."

I ask her where she gets that idea. She says nothing. But I know what she is thinking, going back to earlier conversations we've had. She knows about my support of same-sex marriage, about my acceptance of divorce. "You're a cafeteria Catholic," she said once. I bit my tongue, thinking of her belief in strict immigration laws and deportation of "illegals." I could easily say the same thing about her.

We stand outside the abortion clinic. We do not hold signs; we simply pray the rosary. Making my way through the Sorrowful Mysteries—all focused on Jesus's suffering and death—I remember a recent conversation with a staunchly pro-choice older woman who argued that the rights of a pregnant woman trump those of an unborn fetus. It saddened me to think that such a conflict should have to arise in the first place, a situation where a mother's and child's interests are at odds. How would the world need to change to make such a conflict go away, or at least be less frequent? How would all of us need to be different?

We continue our prayers as people walk in and out of the clinic. We do not try to stop them. I pray for the women, for whatever unknown life circumstances have brought them to this place. And I pray for the children growing inside them, children who may or may not be about to feel a terrible pain, who may or may not know that they are losing their chance to grow up in this world of light and darkness, deep sorrow and unspeakable joy.

~

It's late in the afternoon. Yolanda's appointment is over. She opted for a chemical abortion rather than a surgical one; she has taken one pill at the clinic and will take the other at home in two days. I promise to be there for her in case anything goes wrong, and also to bring her back to her follow-up appointment in two weeks' time.

The late-autumn sun is already setting, and the protesters have gone home. We get in the car and begin the drive back toward our own town. Within minutes, she is asleep.

As we make our way down the country roads, I think of her situation. She has spoken a little about the village she came from, the danger posed by gangs. She has told me about her family's decision to send her here, to the United States, to work for at least a few years until the situation settles down. She has narrated her difficult journey—a week of travel by car, bus, truck, and on foot; her swim across the river; the police car waiting on the other side. Six weeks in jail, and then the journey North, to our little Midwestern town where her cousins were waiting for her. She has spoken of her large amount of debt, about her difficulties managing in school when she barely has any idea of what is going on, when the ESL assistant only works with her for a half hour every other day. She has told me about her long shifts in the Mexican restaurant where she works, washing dishes and busing tables for half the federal minimum wage. And, she has told me about her boyfriend, whom she knew back in Honduras and reconnected with here. She hopes that eventually they will marry, buy some land back home, have children. But not yet.

I cringe as we pass another dead deer at the roadside—probably the tenth instance of road kill I've seen on this trip. She is so intact, so lifelike that I can't see how she was injured. As a relatively new driver who owned a car before moving to the Midwest, I ask myself why we have allowed ourselves to create a society that allows this kind of absurd death of animals to happen every day. Glancing to my right, I notice that Yolanda's eyes have opened briefly. I can only imagine what she is thinking before she falls back to sleep.

Just before we pull onto the interstate, I gasp at a billboard hanging above us. There's an image of an unborn child in the womb. Below it is a phrase I find all too familiar: *A person is a person, no matter how small.* My insides constrict; my hands clam up as I clench the steering wheel more tightly, focusing my gaze steadily on the road ahead. But an image is dancing before my eyes, an image of fourteen-year-old me in a K-Mart-purchased dress and that pro-life button.

Thinking of the abortion debate—still ongoing nearly five decades after abortion was legalized in this country—I can't help but feel that both sides have lost touch with the reality of the human lives involved. Those on the pro-choice side, determined that this is a case where the law cannot rule in a matter of individual conscience, often deny the truth that, yes, abortion does entail the willful, premeditated killing of an unborn child. At the same time, those who call themselves pro-life, with their focus on legislating against abortion while doing nothing to provide concrete help for mothers of young children, so often fail to see the personhood of a woman facing an unplanned pregnancy. Her circumstances are dismissed; almost always, whether subtly or not so subtly, a shameful stigma is placed upon her sexuality. If a woman chooses not to be a virgin, then she had better accept that her only other possibility is to be a mother.

I wonder what might happen if people on both these sides, at least for a day, were to put down their signs, turn off their computers, leave petitions unsigned and legislative representatives uncalled. If they were to meet Yolanda and hear her story, how might their perspective change?

As we turn onto the interstate, I return to that prayer which has always brought me consolation in times of difficulty. Deciding that this day has already contained enough sorrow, I opt for the Rosary's joyful mysteries: Annunciation, Visitation, Nativity, the Presentation of Jesus in the Temple at infancy, and the finding of him there as a twelve-year-old prodigy preacher. I pray for my cousin, the West Point graduate, and all of his fellow soldiers in Afghanistan; I also pray for the people—surely many children among them—whom they have killed. I pray for the people suffering from gang violence in Honduras and Chicago. I pray for Yolanda, Joaquina, and all the undocumented people living in the U.S. and other countries today, all those who have left their homes for fear of violence and abject poverty. I pray for the unborn children who go through abortion, and all the women who have felt the need to make that choice. *A person is a person.* We are all people. We are all frail and needful, cruel and kind; we all stand in need of mercy, dignity, and love.

My Better-Late-Than-Never Confirmation

Sofia Zocca

I. Pleni Sunt Caeli et Terra Gloria Tua

Sitting in bed, cross-legged, cocooned in white pillows, I said my prayers to my nonna. Not "I said my prayers" the way Shirley Temple does in movies, where she kneels by the side of her bed with her hands clasped, eyes closed, and prays that Mama will stay healthy and Daddy will return from war. Not the kind where an adult is always standing in a doorway, watching an orphan pray for a family, magically unheard by the kid despite being about five feet away, in full sight, and tragically sighing with a soft sorrowful smile and pitying eyes. No, the prayers I said with my nonna every night were some hard-core, fully memorized Roman Catholic penitential prayers in Italian. You know in movies when the washed-up protagonist goes to Confession for the first time since he was maybe ten and confesses to "impure thoughts" or ludicrous things to be telling a Catholic priest, and the priest tells the anguished sinner to say five Hail Marys and three Our Fathers? Well, imagine the protagonist actually went home and recited them onscreen instead of just feeling let off the hook for whatever he or she had done because an old man in a full-length robe doled out busywork. Those are the types of prayers I said every night. I said my "padre nostros" and my "Ave Marias" and a few "Gloria al padres," and I even had memorized "Credo," the "Nicea-Costantinopoli" version, which, for all of you who did not happen to spend every summer and Christmas in Formello, Italy, with your good Catholic nonna, is the incredibly long prayer that basically tells the story of Jesus's crucifixion and begins with "*Credo in un solo Dio, Padre onnipotente, Creatore del cielo e della terra, di tutte le cose visibili e invisibili,*" which in English means, "I believe in one God, Father Almighty, maker of heaven and earth, of all that is seen and unseen." Yeah, it's the stuff of *The DaVinci Code*. I recited these every night, and every time I fully learned a prayer, my nonna taught me a new one. I ended each prayer with a proud "*cosìsia*," the amen-esque finish.

Leaning against my throne of plump pillows, having performed my duty as a young Catholic girl and a devoted granddaughter—and honestly I enjoyed the feeling of accomplishment of knowing and successfully delivering my prayers—I told my nonna that she should be a priest. She smiled and patted my hand.

"I can't be a priest," she replied calmly.

"Why not? You're the best Catholic I know, and you love going to church. You would be such a good priest."

This inability did not seem to be an uncomfortable or inconvenient fact to her. It was just the way things were, and she was explaining it to me because I was a little kid who didn't yet understand the world.

"Women can't be priests."

"But why?"

"They just can't."

II. Nativity

I asked Nonna why God made war and people who are mean to each other. It wasn't that I doubted the existence of God or didn't like Catholicism. I mean, I hated sitting through Mass and I used to be unable to sit still. I would play games in my head, like the games I played with my Polly Pockets, but it was all imagined, because I couldn't bring toys to church. I sometimes tried really hard to understand the priest, but none of it made much sense to me. Some highlights of the more engaging sermons: Jesus wasn't really born on Christmas, and Mary and Joseph were just living their little life when the angel Gabriel approached Mary.

I always imagined Gabriel as a female angel. In Italian, the angel's name is Gabriele, which is distinctly different from Gabriella, but nevertheless, I always pictured her as a girl angel. I really liked my female Gabriele and used to play with her porcelain effigy as the protagonist of my invented stories on the *presepe* during Christmastime. I helped Nonna set up the *presepe* every Christmas. Then, I would kneel by the table and play with porcelain Mary and Joseph and Gabriele. Not the birth of Jesus story, mind you. In fact, it needn't have been Christianity-specific characters; I just thought of the *presepe* animals and houses and people as my dolls. I played with them all throughout December, but the most exciting part was getting to move the three wise men a little closer to Mary and Joseph every day, rearranging them so slightly but particularly on their journey to Christmas, until finally I could place them crowded around the crib. On Christmas morning, I took Jesus out of his box and laid him in his basket. It was like playing God with tiny fragile people.

I sat cross-legged on the prickly carpet in the hallway and crumpled newspapers from a pile on the floor next to me. There was an art to crumpling the newspapers so that when I arranged them on the table designated for the *presepe* and covered them with a white sheet, the scene would look like snowy mountains. Next to the newspapers sat the old cardboard box that Nonna carried up from the basement every December. I gently pulled out the wooden hut and the porcelain yellow shack with the orange roof, and I inspected them for cracks. I meticulously placed each balled-up newspaper and uncoiled the fake grass. I wished that I could make the angel really fly, and I concocted elaborate ways to hang her from string. I had garnered these grand ideas about Nonna's and my *presepe* from our yearly visits to Rome's *presepe* displays. These Roman Nativity scenes featured tens of the most beautiful and elaborate set-ups, complete with moving merchants churning butter in a mechanical circular motion over and over, and donkeys that pulled carts along a projected trajectory.

However, my *presepe* games were probably more influenced by my favorite movie, *Opopomoz*. This movie told the story of a little Neapolitan boy, Rocco, who enters the *presepe* in order to stop the birth of Jesus because, somehow, that will prevent the birth of his baby brother, of whom he is already jealous. Now, the reason Rocco enters the *presepe* in the first place is because Satan has sent the three most endearing little devils to manipulate him into it. Of course, the movie ends with Rocco defeating Satan and realizing that the birth of his baby brother is a good thing, and baby Jesus gets to be born. But I didn't particularly care about the Jesus storyline. I always loved the three little devils. They were kind of like Bartok from *Anastasia*, lovable and foolish and with the names Farfaricchio, Scarapino, and Astarotte, which I always heard as "Astanotte," which means "until tonight." Now that I've learned his real name, I'm not sure he's my favorite anymore. But honestly, if the movie's goal was to make kids not listen to the devil, I'm not sure why they created the most likeable devils since Faustus's Mephistopheles. These devils were so ridiculous that they sang the apotropaic nursery rhyme to ward off *themselves* because they thought the tune was catchy. I felt tension watching the end of the movie, because I worried that my beloved devils wouldn't succeed in their task and Satan would be angry with them. I sat up straight, leaning in close to the television, silently hoping for Jesus's abortion.

I asked Nonna, "If God controls everything, then why does war exist?" This is probably a common question among Catholic children because she had an answer locked and loaded.

"Because He is testing us."

I lay in the dark, quietly, my head resting on Nonna's lap, which smelled so distinctly of her that I can't even describe it. The closest I can get is Italian eucalyptus in a Formello garden mixed with tradition, and the air in side streets of older Italian cities, and a hint of established wealth and probably royal status had this been feudal Europe. My half-drunk mint syrup–infused milk comforted me from the wooden bedside table.

"Oh, okay."

I wasn't fully satisfied with this explanation, but Nonna's word was as good as God's.

III. Preview

During my summers and Christmases in Italy, I spent time with my nonno by painting a mural of a sunrise with him on the garage door; I spent time with Matteo playing foosball and laughing at his rendering of a sportscaster; I spent time with Eleonora looking up at her while she read to me from *Brividi*, the Italian translation of the *Goosebumps* books; I spent time with Zia Nicoletta pretending to cook her steak and fry her French fries in my plastic restaurant. But the time Nonna and I spent together, just the two of us, her attention undivided by cooking or cleaning or watching the tiny TV in the kitchen, or being tired and needing to lie down, was going to weekday evening Mass in the small church down the road. For Sunday Mass, the whole family had to go. But weekday nights, only Nonna was devout enough to attend. Because it's not only children who don't enjoy Mass; it's everyone. Everyone, that is, except my nonna. And while Sundays are required church days, weekdays only involve some low-level guilt tripping.

After Mass, when I was seven years old, she walked me up to the priest, who was also her close personal friend.

"*Salve,* Luisa," he greeted her.

She has a stern, downturned mouth that sits still and unamused most of the time, but she blushed and looked down as her lips fought against an inevitable smile as the priest welcomed us. It was the face I most associate with the pencil sketch that her husband drew of her, the one in black and white, in which she fills the frame without any unnecessary background distractions, the one that hangs on the wall beside the first staircase leading up to the second floor of my grandparents' house, the one that's so good it looks like a photograph.

"This is my little granddaughter, Sofia," she told him, her hand perched against my back.

"Nice to meet you, Sofia."

I looked up at him with only my eyes, but was too shy to smile or frown or really respond in any way other than allowing him to take my hand and shake it. The adults talked for a while about the Mass, and Nonna asked the priest how his health had been. A woman approached the priest, and polite as he was, he turned to wish her goodbye and exchange a few words with her. I pulled my grandmother's arm to invite her down to my height, and I stood on my tiptoes, and whispered in her ear. I kept hold of her hand, safekeeping my own inside hers.

She answered me, "We'll see, *tesoro.*" Nonna always called me her treasure.

Once the priest had turned back to us, and the church had emptied, he led us around to give me a tour of the church, which was a modest one room so "tour" is probably a strong word. He walked with us to a small painting hanging on the left wall, facing the pulpit.

"Your nonno painted this," he told me.

"*My* nonno? Really?"

I couldn't believe that my nonno was famous enough to be commissioned by the homey little church of Formello, the only church I enjoyed attending. Really, the only church I could understand attending. The few times my dad took me to churches in America, they were large and loud and filled with dirty bright yellow light. This church was a small, perfectly square-shaped box; the pews had wooden kneelers with nothing soft to cover them; and my nonna knew every single congregant and every single congregant's grandchild.

The priest walked us back to the pulpit in the front, and my nonna relayed to him my request.

"She just really likes the wafers."

He laughed. "I can get you some wafers that I haven't consecrated yet."

He led us to the tiny claustrophobic back room, then opened a door and disappeared into an even more secretive door. We were the distinguished and exclusive members of the tiny-room-in-the-back-of-the-church club, and I was a VIP by proxy of my nonna. The priest returned, bringing with him a deep bowl filled with unconsecrated wafers. They looked the same as the consecrated wafers to me, but I didn't question it. I didn't even fully understand why I couldn't stand up and take Communion yet, but my nonna always told me to "wait here," and while I sat in the pew, she passed by me and got in line and took Communion with the rest of the church. I watched the line move, the only moment of commotion during the entirety of Mass, and I watched Nonna, usually my Catholic heroine, become reduced to an aged hunchbacked woman with her arms by her sides and her tongue sticking out to submissively receive a wafer that seemed to stick to and coalesce into it. Communion was the only time Nonna left me alone in the pew, the only time we weren't experiencing Mass together.

I sat in the tiny, airless room and snacked on tasteless, pasty, white circles that melted in my mouth. I was really on the inside now. And the inner circle got pre-transubstantiation wafers.

IV. Confession, Communion, and Agita

I turned back to face the pulpit for a moment while I crossed myself, imitating my nonna, before leaving the church. We passed through the enclosed lightless room of limbo between the church and outside. I had to lean my entire weight against the second door, only to topple out into the dim white light of evening. I could see my breath in front of me, and my puffy uninsulated coat did little to keep me from feeling cold. I hopped, double-time, to the car, trying not to pull Nonna too fast. On the way home in the car, she resumed my Latin lessons. I was still learning the tenses for the verb "to rise," which my nonna recited perfectly—*orior, oriris, oritur*—over and over because she had had them drummed into her in primary school. The indoctrination didn't work so well for me, and to this day I don't know any Latin.

After dinner, I sat at my usual bench at the wooden table in the kitchen with Nonna, watching her circle the rim of the cake pan with her finger, then lick the bits of crumb and custard from the homemade *torta della nonna*. The overhead lamp hung low over our heads, illuminating the cake in the center of the table.

"Why don't you just eat a slice?" My nonno had made a rare entrance into the kitchen, and grumbled at my nonna in irritation.

"No, no, I don't want a slice."

"I don't want a slice, she says, as she licks the crumbs from the cake."

I giggled, amused by my nonno, and my nonna blushed and withdrew her hand. She asked me if I wanted another piece, and I enthusiastically nodded, my whole tiny body moving in excitement. Nonna stood up and brought the cake to the sink, her back turned to Nonno and me.

"Are you coming to Mass with us tomorrow, Nonno?" I asked him.

"No. You go with your nonna."

"He doesn't come to Mass," Nonna said teasingly from the sink. My nonno furrowed his face in aggravation and paced from the doorway to the drawer by the TV. He began to fidget noisily around in the drawer, I suppose looking for something.

"Nonna is so good, she goes to Mass every day," I chimed in, proud that I knew that going to Mass equaled being a good person. Nonno slammed the drawer, glared and threw a "come on, Luisa!" at Nonna, and stormed from the kitchen.

That night, lying on my sheets with my chin on my palms and feet flailing in the air, I watched Nonna bring a thick cardboard book with pictures into my room. She sat at the edge of the bed and leaned back against my quilt and read to me from the book. The story of Noah's Ark wasn't as fun and full of cartoon animals as I had thought. It was way more about God's punishment and destruction of the world, without a heavy emphasis on colorful giraffes and flamingos walking two by two onto a nice cruise. I had to memorize these stories for my First Communion in the spring, which took all the fun of reading out of the whole process. The most frustrating part to Nonna was that I couldn't understand why God would save Noah.

"Why does Noah get to live?"

"Because God chose him."

"But why is *he* so special?"

I thought it was pretty nonsensical, especially considering the comical way I saw the animals in my mind. I colorized and animated them. I played the cartoon for my nonna, laughing uncontrollably when I described them as they appeared in my head. She was not as amused. In my imagination, all the animals took their sweet time strolling onto the deck of a cruise ship, discussing the sunny weather, perhaps carrying parasols, a little like the passengers on the *Titanic*.

~

I sat in the kitchen on Saturday afternoon, while Nonna peeled and sliced green apples into thick fat wedges and handed them to me. I ate them happily. I always got hungry around four in the afternoon, and dinner wasn't until at least eight.

"What will my First Communion be like?"

My nonna smiled approvingly at this topic and turned so that she could face me, while still holding the knife and apple over the sink as she cut reflexively.

"Well, you'll be wearing your white dress and the veil that I bought you, and your father will walk you to the priest. You'll say the prayer you've been memorizing, and the priest will give you your first consecrated wafer."

Nonna had already bought me my white dress and white gloves for the day that she had told everyone was very special to me. It was the only day I wore them, and I never saw them again. The most memorable part of that "special day" was that we were running late. Nonna was already at the church by the time we pulled up. She was standing by the side of her car, arms crossed and lips tight. My dad slammed on the brakes in the middle of a small side road and told me to get out. I ran out and skipped over to my nonna, my white dress trailing in the grime of the road. My father parallel parked more rapidly and less accurately than I had ever seen and ran over to me, hunched down with his arms outstretched and a wide smile.

"Let's go!"

"The priest has been waiting," Nonna hissed at my father.

I had been so nervous about forgetting my lines, but in all the commotion I completely forgot to be nervous about messing up in front of everyone. Instead the gutted feeling in my stomach twisted into *agita* because of my family in the side street in front of the church.

In preparation for my First Communion, I made my First Confession. It was with Nonna's priest friend, so I was a little worried he would tell my nonna if I confessed anything bad. He seemed to expect me to have done worse things at seven than I even knew about.

"Do you ever say bad words?"

"No," I answered. Truthfully, I couldn't bring myself to say bad words even if I had wanted to, even though I knew bad words from the other kids in school.

But after a few questions with "no" for answers, I began to feel like he either didn't believe me or I was a little disappointing as a confessor. After all, the point of Confession was to tell the priest all the terrible things you've done, and if you answer "no" to all their questions, how can it really be any fun for them?

But then he asked me if I ever lied, and I knew I had to say yes. I had had an assignment for school to draw a picture of "something that represents your culture." So I drew Leonardo da Vinci's *The Last Supper*, revised to include the female Italian members of my family: Nonna, Zia Nicoletta, Zia Paola, and my cousin Eleonora. My teacher called it "sacrilegious," and her tone implied that this was not a compliment, so when my nonna asked me to mail her what I had drawn, I told her that I never got the picture back. The priest asked me if I knew "Ave Maria," and I told him I did. He sent me off with the Penance to say two "Ave Marias." Penance is the "Get Out of Jail Free" card for Catholics. Even the most hardened murderer Catholic knows an "Ave Maria."

He walked me back out to where Nonna was waiting for me. Instead of feeling absolved of sin and forgiven like I was promised, I felt ashamed, as if I now had a secret with this priest I barely knew, which we were keeping from Nonna. *He* could know that I lied, but my own nonna couldn't? She knew I had just been talking about sin, but she didn't know what we had talked about specifically. It was the first time I had really had a secret from Nonna.

As we walked back to the car, Nonna asked me if I had any homework. I told her I had to say two "Ave Marias" but it was with extreme trepidation, because *now* she wouldn't know *why* I had to say these "Ave Marias," and she would imagine that I'd done the worst. She wouldn't know what I'd done, but she'd know I had done something wrong if the priest was telling me to say two "Ave Marias."

But her voice was calm and even:

"You can say them tonight when we say our usual prayers."

That afternoon in the kitchen, before all the trouble with the two "Ave Marias," while I bit into my juicy apple chunks, I thought about all Nonna's stories of saints and whether I would ever become one. It seemed awfully arbitrary that these random people got to be saints. We were big celebrants of the *onomastico,* your saint's name day. Being named Sofia, and being a Roman girl myself, like my saint buddy, I felt an even greater kinship to Santa Sofia. On your day, everyone would get together and wish you "*buon onomastico,*" which is pretty exciting because it's like getting a second birthday. My nonno's birthday was actually on September 30, the same day as my *onomastico,* and we always celebrated them together with cake.

"How do people get to be saints?"

Nonna hesitated, then replied, "They have to do something really good."

"Like what?"

"Like save someone's life. They have to be really good, and they have to be able to make miracles happen."

Always the pragmatist, I needed specifics: "How many miracles do you have to do before you get to count as a saint?"

Nonna smirked, but she humored me. "I'd say three."

"Okay," I resolved, "I'll do three miracles and then I'll be a saint."

Being a saint would be pretty neat: you'd get to lord it over people, and you'd get to be remembered forever as someone holy.

I thought for a while about what miracles I could perform, but in the end, I decided that it would be best to figure out what my specific powers were before attempting any miracles. I could save someone's life, easy. Although then there'd be two Santa Sofias, and that might be confusing for God. Already it was awkward enough when there was a Sophia in one of my classes, and having the same name with the same *spelling* for all eternity might create some competition between me and my namesake.

V. Mortality and Doubt

The following Thursday, Nonna and I went to evening Mass again. There were many fewer people during the weekday services, and it was a lot colder and darker and emptier and even draftier during evening Mass. But I liked going to evening Mass even better than Sunday Mass because it meant I was doing something extra. I was good like my nonna. At the part when the priest tells everyone to turn to the person on your left and your right and wish them peace, I always turned to Nonna first. I laughingly shook her hand and did an over-the-top "*pace.*" I felt like I was getting away with something because I already knew her. Although on that Thursday, I also already knew the person on my right. She was Nonna's friend. Her church friend, of course. This made it a lot less stressful to shake her hand and made me a lot less timid about speaking to a stranger. We were supposed to stand while we shook our neighbors' hands and made peace. I hated the standing parts, but I liked the kneeling parts, because it gave me something to do.

After the service, we went over to the pulpit where the priest stood, and he and my nonna talked. A few minutes into their conversation, he put his hand to his forehead.

"I feel faint . . ."

"Are you okay, Father?" Nonna asked, becoming concerned.

The priest appeared to lose focus. His face was pale and sweating, and he was losing balance, his entire body moving in a slight counterclockwise rotation.

"Do you need water?"

"Yes, I'll just get some water."

We followed him over to his tiny room, it was the size of a pantry really, and he opened the door, showing his entire sanctuary to the church. Everyone had left by now, as it was well into evening. He was a spry man, in seemingly perfect health. At least, as perfect as health can be at seventy. Not even two steps into the room, he collapsed onto the floor. Nonna ran to get him water, and she sat with him while he sat up and drank it.

After a few minutes, he seemed better. He was no longer out of control of his own body. He still looked tired, but not like he was about to have a heart attack or a stroke. We sat with him for a long time, and I hated it. I was in a silent fuming rage, and I could barely stand there, still, and not just turn around and leave. The priest couldn't *die*. He was the priest, for Christ's sake. He looked fine every time I saw him; what was this insane turn of events, this insane decision to simply *collapse*? This was so outside the realm of anything that could possibly have happened. Was he now *ill*? Who decided to make *that* happen? I was furious at this incomprehensible series of events, at this illogical procession of time. It was absurd. He couldn't just be my nonna's friend, my well-known priest, my family priest, my confessor, one day, and then suddenly die. You can't be fine your entire existence, and then suddenly just not be. And I had had to watch this powerful man, the actual *priest*, fall like a little baby. Could the church even go on existing if he died? I mean, he was the priest. If he dies, what happens to his church? I wanted to know who had okayed this. I wanted to demand accountability and damages for making me watch this and then again for making me sit there while he, I don't know, caught his breath? Can you just collapse and then all you need is to catch your breath? That's not a *thing* that happens. I couldn't conceptualize *why* he would do this, and *why* I had to be there to witness it happening.

VI. Reckoning

Nonna called me at around two in the afternoon, eight in the evening in Formello, as she did every Sunday when I was home in

America. I was fourteen, and she had a big conversation planned for this particular Sunday in March. I could tell because she kept hesitating and pausing, and she kept getting distracted and not responding to my news about the school play and my gossip about the cast. "Nonna? Did you hear me?" "Oh yes, yes, *tesoro,* sorry, I heard you, yes." Finally, I had no more to say and we sat on the phone in silence for about eight seconds.

"Sofia . . . when are we going to start the discussion of your Confirmation?"

I instinctively winced, while my entire body held itself suspended in tension. I didn't know what to say.

"Nonna? I have a question."

"Tell me, *tesoro.*"

"When did you know . . . *for sure* that God exists?"

She sighed. "I still don't, *tesoro.* But I choose to believe that He does. You know, Confirmation isn't about knowing anything for sure. There will never come a time when you can know. You don't just turn fourteen, or eighteen, or twenty-one, or even seventy-eight, and suddenly you know everything, and you're sure of everything, and you have all the answers. You know? There's no proof, but I choose to believe."

That evening, I looked out my window and tried to find a star that looked symbolic and melodramatic enough to be a proper wishing star. Like in *Annie* or *Miracle on 34th Street.* And I prayed that I would believe in God, even though to me the stars all looked the same.

VII. Twitch Upon the Thread

Watching *Jane the Virgin* every Friday night while eating a veggie burger is probably my only Catholic activity. That and maybe making God jokes, followed by a retraction with an only somewhat flippant "God's gonna smite me for that." I ride down to Rome on the train from Florence in the sweltering summer heat. I have two paperbacks in my backpack: Susanna Tamaro's *Va' dove ti porta il cuore,* which Nonna had given me, and an Evelyn Waugh novel that I had brought with me from America, and in which I had highlighted this passage:

"I caught him, with an unseen hook and an invisible line which is long enough to let him wander to the ends of the world, and still to bring him back with a twitch upon the thread."

I arrive at the Roma Termini train station and I look through the dense crowd swarming around trying to find their loved ones on the platform. Through the mass of people, I see a little trio of stern-faced expectants, weary in the face and looking out and through the crowds of people the way you do when anxiously waiting for someone. I walk toward them. The man, tall, thick hair, and a strong jaw, smiles and waves. The woman, curly dark hair, knowingly grinning eyes, and eye bags much more sunken than when I had last seen her, cracks open her mouth into a wide smile and outstretches her arms to me. The third person, standing in front of the couple, hunched over at about 4'10" with lines pulling her lips down into a frown, makes no movement, but continues to look out through the crowd. I have walked all the way up to them by the time she exclaims, "Ahh! Sofia!" She embraces me, and I stiffly and awkwardly acquiesce. My *zia* Nicoletta scurries over to me and pulls me into a warm, all-encompassing hug.

"Let me hug her, she's my niece!"

"Yes, but she's my granddaughter, and the granddaughter-grandmother relationship is the more important one."

My *zio* Corrado sits back amusedly and watches the women take turns hugging me. Once they have stepped back and we begin walking out of the station, he hugs me and greets me with a casual, but expressive, "Hi, Sofia, how've you been?"

We reach the car, and Zio Corrado loads my one backpack into the trunk.

"That's it?" my nonna asks, concerned.

"Yes, Nonna, that has everything I need."

Nonna tells me to sit in the back with her: "I want my little granddaughter to sit with me. I never get to see her!"

But Zio Corrado insists that I will be more comfortable in the front, so Nonna concedes the point, and I sit by my *zio,* who drives us through the busy, jaywalking, loud, bustling Roma Termini crowds. Stopping short to avoid hitting a group of pale, blonde girls running across the street, my *zio* yells out his window at them.

"Roma is full of tourists. They all just run across the street and have no respect for our city."

"Yeah, tourists are the worst," I agree.

"You don't just come to our city and disrespect all our laws and do whatever you want. You just don't do that."

I tell him that I don't really remember there being this many tourists when I was younger. I guess it's because we didn't really do much sightseeing. We once drove past the Colosseum, which my dad pointed out to me as he briefly explained its history. And I loved going to Piazza Navona and Piazza di Spagna and especially the Fontana di Trevi. But other than brief excursions into the city if we wanted to go out for a pizza dinner with the family, or to visit my cousins in their tiny, cramped three-bedroom apartment with narrow hallways, we mostly stayed at my grandparents' house in Formello, or in the shopping center near their house where the church was located.

Nonna surprisedly observes that my Italian is still so good.

"Of course," Zio Corrado responds, his arm on the back of my seat, turning around to look out of the right backseat window as he backs up to turn around, "it's her mother tongue, you never forget that."

As we approach the base of a series of steep hills, Nonna explains that we are going to my Zia Nicoletta and Zio Corrado's. When we arrive, Zia Nicoletta runs in to finish heating up the dinner she has been preparing for me all day.

"If you don't like anything, don't feel like you have to eat it. Just eat what you want," Nonna tells me as she claims her seat next to me at the table. There's salmon and eggplant parmesan and asparagus and thinly sliced roast beef. There are a lot more vegetables than when I was little and we used to eat tortellini al brodo or lasagna or gnocchi every night. But what shocks me most is the roast beef. It's a Friday night. I had never in my life been with my nonna and eaten meat on a Friday. Fridays we either had a heavier first course, or fish for the second. It was simply a given that meat would not be bought, served, or eaten if it were a Friday. For a long time, I had thought that it was a worldwide rule that everyone *had* to follow.

Nonna does not eat the meat, but to even allow it at the table. . . . To not mention that she wasn't eating it, or explain why, or otherwise acknowledge it. She passes the dish to me without seeming to think twice.

"How's college?" Zio Corrado asks me.

"It's pretty good . . . I have one more year."

"Only one more year, really?!" Nonna looks up from her food.

"Yeah, I know, it's crazy," I laugh nervously.

Zia Nicoletta sighs and squeezes me in her arms.

"My little niece is getting so grown up. Soon you're going to have a job and a house and you'll be getting married."

Actually, I don't want to get married, I think to myself. One virginal white dress and long church ceremony at my First Communion was enough for me. Plus, marriage adds the whole property sale from father to husband thing into the mix, and I didn't particularly want to practice a spirituality or a femininity that included patriarchal hierarchy. But this was a discussion that I didn't want to have with my nonna. She didn't need to hear me undermine every tradition she had raised me to respect.

We spend the night at Zia Nicoletta and Zio Corrado's. I wake up before everyone else the next morning and wander through the small apartment in the natural sunlight. Once everyone has risen, we eat breakfast. In the fresh light, no longer sleep-deprived from my train ride, I notice the panel of framed black-and-white photographs on the wall behind me. Global social justice activists, including Mahatma Gandhi, Antonio Gramsci, and Martin Luther King Jr., stare back at me. I compliment my *zia* and *zio* on the chosen leaders, to which Zia Nicoletta responds,

"It's your Zio Corrado's, not mine. There are no women in the photos. He only likes men."

Zio Corrado rolls his eyes and smirks. No one mentions the small picture of the Pope—another man, of course—off to the side of the panel: the staple of every Italian household, practicing or not.

We slowly get ready to go to my cousins' other nonna's house out in the country. My nonna explains the plan for the day to me. As we leave the apartment, Zia Nicoletta fills a tote bag that reads "women who vote," which she purposely holds up to Zio

Corrado, who swats her away with a distracted, "alright, enough." We are running late, but we stop quickly to pick up the quintessential *pastine mignon* that mark every lunch with my family. We eat lunch there, accompanied by Zio Alberto's parodied "*namo a magna*" in romanesco, and it's not until 4:30 in the afternoon that we slowly, calmly meander out of the driveway, after a million kisses and hugs, crushing gravel as we pull out toward the gate at the end of the estate.

Zio Corrado is driving, as usual, but this time I sit in the back with my nonna, who holds her arm linked through mine. Nonna informs me that we are finally going back to her house to spend the night. Throughout the sleepy afternoon car ride, she reports that Ele has her graduation from la Sapienza in June—either June 8th or 10th—and did I know that Zio Alberto was sick? Yes, he was very sick, but he's been better for two years now, but that's why he looks like he's aged so much. And Andrea just got a job in technology, but he hates it, and Matteo likes computer science too, and Andrea is much more methodical, he really follows the rules in figuring out technological issues, but Matteo just goes for it and makes a mess, but sometimes that's what works best in computer science. And Ele wants to go to school for journalism now, but it's very competitive, but that's what she wants to do, and she spent a semester in Holland, but she hated it, it was very dark and very cold, and she went to Japan for a semester as well and she really liked that. She studied Japanese in university but now she wants to study journalism.

We pull up to the gate that guards Nonna's and her neighbors' houses. Zio Corrado enters the passcode, and we crunch over the gravel road that leads us to Nonna's. We all get out of the car, and Zio Corrado insists on carrying my backpack inside for me. He takes the key hanging hidden under vines on the brick wall and opens the gate to my grandparents' property.

I walk down the brick pathway, surrounded by my grandparents' Edenic garden, the perfect hide and seek place for children. I feel my muscle memory lead me to the door, past the plastic encasing full of cacti, past the ceramic-potted orchids that line the walkway. Reds and greens bring the old house to life, and I stand at the heavy front door. Zio Corrado takes out his keychain and fumbles through the keys to get the right one.

"Don't walk in yet," Zia Nicoletta tells me, her hand across my shoulders.

After turning the key in the lock, Zio Corrado strides swiftly into the house, crosses the hall to a plastic box on the wall, the only part of the house I don't recognize, and types in a security code. "Okay, we can go in now," Zia Nicoletta gently leads me into the house, her arm still situated around me. I pause in the doorway, the entire house before me. My *zia, zio,* and nonna pass me, place my backpack on a chair in the hallway, and enter the kitchen. The long, intricately detailed maroon rug runs through the hallway to a shiny black step down to the living room, composed of two couches and a hidden corner, invisible from my angle. Looking up, I see the wraparound indoor balcony. My face feels wet, and in my chest, a sharp pain strikes.

I walk straight into the downstairs bathroom and look in the mirror. I carefully swipe my finger along the waterline of each eye, smile at my reflection, and walk out. I turn the corner and walk into the kitchen. The walls, which I didn't even realize you could write on, are now filled with phone numbers and all-caps REMEMBER TOs in my zia Nicoletta's handwriting. I cross to the sink and open the cabinet door to throw away my tissue.

"You still remember where the trashcan is!" Nonna exclaims, visibly impressed.

"Oh . . . yeah, I guess so," my body, remembering its old habits, must have brought me to the trashcan without my brain realizing it.

Zia Nicoletta and Zio Corrado leave, and it is the first time Nonna and I have been alone all weekend. She brings out a light dinner of prosciutto, mozzarella di bufala, and cantaloupe.

"I remember how much you always loved mozzarella di bufala. You loved it more than anyone I've ever known. You used to know whether it was mozzarella di bufala or not just by tasting it."

After dinner, she pulls out a box of cornetto popsicles from the freezer—"you always loved these, do you still like them?"—and

I savor one as we exit the house through the kitchen door and stroll down the brick pathway to the garage.

"You and your nonno painted this together, do you remember?"

I smile because of course I remember. It's faded and chipping, but the bright red sun peeking out of the mountaintop under a rainbow is still perfectly clear. We stand in the mosquito-filled evening air for a few minutes before turning around and walking back up to the kitchen.

Nonna asks if I want to watch some television in the living room, and I do. I just need to check something on the computer first. I enter my nonno's study, where a computer sits and has sat for approximately one hundred years. If I had to guess, I'd say it's the biggest computer still in existence. The wooden desk next to it is covered in scattered papers. One of them catches my attention. It's a small rectangular white flyer. A picture of my nonno smiling down toward the corner of the page features prominently. "In loving memory, Attilio Zocca." A giant cross and the address of the church appear below his name. I had received the SMS text two-and-a-half years ago, and I can't seem to muster any tears now either. I just stare at the flimsy paper. Nineteenth-century literature often uses the trope of the reformed villain who has an epiphany and gets forgiven by God at the end of the novel right before he dies. But I don't think that works as well when a lapsed Catholic wants forgiveness and isn't dying, and wasn't even at the dead person's funeral.

Leaving the study, I join Nonna on the couch by the television. A European Cup soccer game is on. Italy versus Germany. If Italy wins, they will be eligible to go to the finals, but if they lose, they're out.

"You're not Catholic anymore, are you?"

VIII. The Catechism—The Operation of Grace

You know, just because you don't believe in God doesn't mean you don't believe in anything or that you aren't spiritual. Lots of people believe in sending out good energy or in some sort of karmic power that encourages them to be kind to others. Or what about compassion and empathy? Shouldn't that be considered a better reason to be a good person than the threat of Hell or the promise of Heaven? Shouldn't we feel more accountable to other humans than to God? The most selfish reason I could possibly imagine for "doing the right thing" would be that I was promised a perfect world if I do. That's not morality, or ethics; that's pure rational choice theory. I mean, Catholicism is pretty genius. How do we get people to follow rules we want, some including ethical behavior that we think is good to teach people, like treating others the way you want to be treated, some that probably had a purpose when the Bible was written, and some that are just serving the self-interest of rich old white men, like no sex until marriage? We make them believe in God and then tell them that God said so.

I think Catholicism is making a bit of a comeback now with the cool Pope Francis. Even Bernie Sanders, a Jewish democratic socialist politician from Brooklyn, quotes Pope Francis. How much cooler can someone get, really, than being re-tweeted by Bernie Sanders? But I'd just like to point out that the Pope's headshot had been prominently featured in every room in every Italian household since way before Pope Francis and "cool Catholicism." Who's the trendsetter now? Although, Bernie's agreement with Pope Francis really shows a possibility for spirituality and spiritual solidarity outside of the limitations set by male-originated organized religion.

Unable to sleep, I annotate Aemilia Lanyer's *Salve Deus Rex Judæorum* under the dark light of the bedside lamp, which balances on a light pink crocheted doily. I will be writing about Aemilia for my senior thesis in the upcoming academic year, and as I read through the poem, I think that maybe she had it all figured out back in 1611. She reconciled religion and feminism and social justice by advocating for a community of pious women. She hoped to achieve intergenerational female solidarity and transcend class distinctions through unified prayer and religious study. For Aemilia, spirituality allows women to unite and to enter political, religious, and sociocultural discourses. Aemilia writes her entire poem as a Eucharist to be consumed by women occupying different socioeconomic statuses—she would never have wanted my nonna to take

Communion without me, to tell me to "wait here," to experience a part of Mass without her granddaughter.

But as I lie in the bed I occupied every summer of my childhood, I can't stop thinking about Nonna's question. I hold the rosary beads that I always carry in the small pocket in my backpack, the ones she had given to me many, many years ago, wound tightly around my left hand. The round borders dip into my palm, simultaneously smooth and hard. The cross rests on top of my fingers. My hand burrowed under the cool pillow, the rosary pressed into my hot hand, I forcefully push my humid face into the pillow. Two Ave Marias come unbidden to my mind.

I assumed we would go to Mass on Sunday, but my nonna slept in and never mentioned it. Leaving the house to be driven back to Roma Termini, I walk up the pathway, yellow grass fighting its way through the cracks in the brick, and I can't look back. I really wish I could, but I just can't work up enough strength or even energy to turn around and force myself to look at the house where I spent my childhood and Catholic upbringing. Maybe it's for the best; maybe I would've turned into a little pillar of salt or something. But I don't really remember much about that story, anyway.

IX. Descent of Spiritus Sanctus

Back in Firenze that night, I open my window to let in some air, and I lean outside. It's dark outside except for a dingy streetlight, so the light from inside my room would illuminate my face to the passers-by outside. Except they never look up. From Piazza Santo Spirito, the square of the Holy Spirit, I hear Umberto Tozzi's "Gloria" blasting:

Gloria
manchi tu nell'aria
manchi come il sale
manchi più del sole
sciogli questa neve
che soffoca il mio petto
t'aspetto Gloria

Let Us Pray Together

Julianne DiNenna

I am the blond who might sit in the car next to yours in the school pick-up zone
but you do not see me, not that anyone would notice me beyond my hair,
I slipped in at the back, starved and dehydrated.

I am the thick-haired curvy-bodied brunette you might knock into at the grocery store
by accident—on a lucky day you might excuse yourself to the shades, notice the hips,
you can't see my purple eggplant eyes, I dart past towing kids and cart.

I am the dark, kinky-haired mother who might clean your house,
whose kids subdue their aches and pains on the playground or in parked cars
while I earn three/fourths of his dollar that he will take from me.

We are the women who have crossed your lines because our borders were double-crossed.
The same hands that once caressed us turned on us,
beat us, burnt cigarettes into our backs, strangled our throats,

Tattooed our faces, beat fists into our breasts, made us beg and talk to the feet
that kicked our bellies in the first, second, and third trimesters,
that knocked us down the stairs, knocked us over overturned chairs,

Held guns to our heads, yanked our hair till it ripped out in their hands,
twisted our wrists behind our backs and preached to beg God.
We are your mothers, your sisters, your cousins, your daughters,

Your grandmothers, your wives, we give birth to your progeniture, we are not statues in blue.
  We are the ones who turn from you in shame, beg for forgiveness sometimes
    when the hand became a fist, when the fist became a foot,

When the foot became—God, we cannot say what blunt object
  split our scalps, sliced our lips, thrashed our teeth,
    spilled blood from our noses, bruised our mouths for speaking.

You are the police stopping us at the border, you are the God every priest tells us to pray to
  at the altar, arresting us and ripping our children away, preaching subservience.
    You will never ask our names, but you will know our husbands, our fathers,

Drink wine with them, break bread with them, collect their coins.
  You would rather have us gagged, raped, gunned down,
    parched along the lowway than save us or shield our children—

And yet, and yet,—there is always a "yet"—
  This Trinity of Police, Priest, Big Brother government barking on about our bodies—
    We carry on carrying kids, refusing your orders, praying for you,
      Saving Ourselves

Part Two

Sexuality and Motherhood

From the Womb of Christ

Pat Brisson

Jesus came to change things.
No more sacrificial lambs were to be left on the altar;
now the Lamb was to be eaten—
so we could become the Lamb
and the Lamb could become us.

Here is Jesus, fully human,
(with an X chromosome)
at His most feminine,
speaking of an intimacy only a woman can fully realize:

"Take this all of you and eat of it
for this is my body which will be given up for you.

Take this all of you and drink from it.
For this is the chalice of my blood,
the blood of the new and eternal covenant . . ."

> I, too, have given up my body for my Beloved
> have sheltered new life in the chalice of my womb
> and fed this life with my very blood.

I, too, have made that covenant like no other—
a blood promise, a sacred oath,
a willingness to sacrifice all for the sake of the other.

Always, everywhere our first Bread was Milk.

This is what it is to be born human—
having been nourished on the blood of the Host
and gathered strength for the journey
to then be pushed out of the nurturing womb
blinking and crying into the light of the world.

This is what it is to be born again—
to leave the bloody nurturing womb of Christ
and to go out into the world following His instructions
to do this in memory of Him:
to love and to love and to love.

Feminism, Faith, and My Mother's Church

Valerie Wexler

I have told my mother I am an atheist twice so far.

It was a realization that came quickly but it took me a while to tell her, the only person who would be affected by this discovery in any significant way. My Jewish atheist dad had never discouraged or encouraged any sort of belief, and I didn't have any seriously religious friends. But my mom had always been Catholic and had always had some hope, I think, that I would return to the church someday.

Recently we discovered old film of her first communion. She fidgets excitedly in her white dress and huge veil, trying to stay appropriately solemn as she is escorted by my grandfather and a small boy in his best suit. As she lines up with the other children she looks for a familiar face. You can't tell if someone called her name on the silent film, but suddenly she sees the camera. Her smile is like my smile. She was on her way to accepting the grace of God into her heart and officially becoming a member of the church, but for her and those children surrounding her, Catholicism had always been an immutable part of life.

For entertainment she read *Lives of the Saints*, immersing herself in the exquisite horror of every martyr's gruesome death.

She lived with constant self-imposed guilt and a deep-seated fear of sinning. She occasionally dreamed of being a nun.

My own faith had never been that solid to begin with. I had taken some pride in my Catholicism and in the ritual and pageantry of attending church, but my belief in God was tenuous. My parents let me decide on my own whether and how to believe, a freedom I will always be grateful for, even if it added more choices to a world that sometimes seemed overwhelmingly full of decisions to be made.

I followed her to Mass every Sunday, in keeping with a compromise made with my nonbelieving dad that meant I didn't go to Sunday school but I did go to church. I was sometimes confused by phrases I heard but didn't ask many questions; I was content to make up my own answers. I once took a pink marker and drew what I thought God looked like—a loosely human-shaped form made up of hearts.

I continued to have a vague but steady faith for a long time, that there was a benevolent someone or some being out there. For all the reasons that have been repeated before and that many continue to believe. How else to explain the beauty of late afternoon sunlight or the mystery of the Fibonacci sequence? I'm sure I was also not the first person to discover that adulthood—and the realization that adults have just as little true clarity about the world around them as children—can make it difficult to trust in anything as straightforward as a higher power. Somewhere along the line, during that progress into adulthood, I lost the ability to believe. I didn't want to stop believing, I just discovered one day that I didn't, like a switch had been flipped. I could still see all that beauty I had perceived in the world, but I could no longer see a pattern in its chaos.

I did not want to disappoint my mom, but also I was irrationally scared of shaking her own faith. Not that I thought she was easily shakable, but because if anyone could do it I could. This woman who interviewed mobsters as a journalist, faced down senators as a public interest lobbyist, and taught me about feminism and to never take shit, can be hurt by me. I know too often I have hurt her, because overwhelming love makes me lash out to keep back feelings so strong I have to clench my fists and cross my arms and stay very still to keep from being consumed—or from causing pain. I worried that if we talked about it, fought about it, she might also lose her ability to believe, a switch would be turned off in her as well.

Of course that didn't happen. My mom's belief in a good and just God is strong and she draws comfort from it in ways I'm not sure I will ever understand.

Her dreams morphed from nun to English critic to journalist. She left her all-girls Catholic high school and went to university in Canada, amazed to discover the male competition her nun teachers had ominously warned her about was so feeble. But her faith stayed. It evolved in some ways as she changed and grew as a person, as her politics became more and more progressive, but it has always been with her.

I had to tell her a second time that I didn't believe in God a few months ago. I realized she had hoped that if she just didn't mention it my faith would come back, like a wound that needed time to heal. She was quiet and then asked, "Do you think I'm a chump for believing?" No, I insisted, and meant it, but I didn't tell her how much I envied her faith. We all want meaning in our lives. Our art, our ancient myths, what else have they ever been but expressions of our search for why we exist and why we should go on existing? What my mother has gotten from her faith is everything I like about religion. The reassurance in feeling like not everything is within your control, the belief there is good in everyone, the community and ritual. Faith like hers, a rational faith in a kind God who provides meaning where none is apparent, is anything but chump-ish.

I have found other things that make my life meaningful and continue to look for more, but faith is a powerful force and I understand my mom's sorrow for my loss of it. I know she will continue to hope, and I may have to tell her a third time, maybe even a fourth or fifth, but that is ok.

It is not her faith that sometimes puzzles me but her church. When she'd return from a service at our conservative Catholic church, fuming because the priest's sermon railed against abortion or gay marriage, or even refused to acknowledge the existence of the new "liberal" Pope Francis, I occasionally asked her why she stays. Why does her belief in God mean sitting and listening to a man representing an institution that seemed to be based on exclusion and disrespect of women?

Her answers never quite satisfied me but I have not pressed my questions because I don't think there will ever be an answer I will fully understand, and my mom does not owe me one. But where I have been timid in confronting those questions, my mother herself has been willing to face them head on. She knew her answers were not enough for me and has wondered at times if they were enough for her. My mom has never denied the many problems she has with the church, but she has not been able to separate her faith and the institution completely. For her, that institution is both incidental and essential to her faith. Her belief in God would remain even if the Catholic Church dissolved tomorrow. But while it lasts it is a necessary component of her belief and of who she is.

I made this attempt to put my conflicted feelings about my mom's religion into words after watching her do the same thing. For the past three years she has interviewed feminist and womanist Catholics, asking them the same questions she has struggled with, collecting their experiences and answers in a book.

In her introduction she writes about what she was seeking: "I wasn't looking for an affirmation of faith; nor was I looking for resistance to it. I just wanted to discover whether the struggles I felt were shared by others. I was on a quest, seeking the answer to a very personal question: Was it possible to be a woman who was an independent thinker, a professional in the workplace, who firmly believed in women's equality, and still be a Catholic?"

The scholars, activists, and survivors she interviewed had no easy answers, but she was not expecting them. She figured out a long time ago how to be both a feminist and Catholic: by simply being a feminist and Catholic. What she was looking for, and what she found, was an acknowledgment of a shared struggle and the determination to not shut her eyes to the conflicts that come with that. By choosing to remain Catholic my mom has been facing her faith and her church head-on every day. It's a choice I could not make, a choice that fewer and fewer daughters are making, but I am glad she has held on to something so important to her.

It is still hard for me to imagine any acceptable answer to questions on reconciling the Catholic faith with feminism. My mother is braver than I, though; she has found her answers, but she is not afraid to keep asking questions.

Raising Valerie

Celia Viggo Wexler

This story is about my own struggle to pass on my faith to my daughter. It is a story repeated in the families of many Catholic feminists. The church will never run out of female members. But it may lose the very women who can reform and change the institution in fundamental ways. We raised our daughters to think for themselves and demand equality. They will not settle for the second-class citizenship as Catholics that many of us have endured all our lives. A church that loses our daughters will be much poorer, denied their intelligence, their passion, and their commitment to social justice, equality, and fairness.

Thirty-three years ago, a very pregnant version of me and a spouse who had a far thicker head of hair spent an evening considering baby names for our first child. We had had no trouble choosing a boy's name. Philip, with its straightforward two syllables, and reduced chances for awkward nicknames, satisfied both of us.

But what if the baby was a girl? That was far more challenging. We both wanted a name that carried a certain gravitas, so that if she became president of the U.S. or a CEO of a large corporation, her name would not be a distraction. We cut from the list Tiffany, Tammy, April, Amber, and I'm sure a whole raft of actresses' names that might have been in vogue back then.

My spouse is Jewish by birth and culture, and proud of his heritage. But he also is an atheist, raised by atheist parents. So we also avoided conspicuously Catholic names, no matter how striking. Cross out Mary, Elizabeth, Margaret, and Teresa in all her varieties.

Our final choice, and one we never came to regret, was Valerie. I liked the way it sounded, and how it blended with our last name. I was happy that her initials would be VW. But what pleased me most was the name's origin: Valerie is the feminine version of the Roman word Valerius, meaning strong or valiant.

My daughter has been strong all her life. From infancy, she had an implacable will. Even as a toddler, it was nearly impossible to distract her from her goals. In truth, she has always been entirely her own person. I had no idea what that would mean when I negotiated the terms of engagement with my husband about Valerie's Catholicism.

Yes, he agreed to baptize her. Yes, she could attend weekly Mass with me. But I agreed not to proselytize. To my husband, that meant spontaneously discussing my Catholic faith. I could, however, answer any question she asked. He said that he would never challenge my beliefs to dissuade her, although he would be free to discuss his own views if she asked.

"No problem," I thought to myself. As she grows up, she'll have a million questions. She'd ask about what she heard and saw at Mass. At Christmas, she was bound to be curious about baby Jesus, an inescapable aspect of celebrating the holidays in the U.S. Even the Rockettes' Christmas show ends with a nativity scene! And then, when a favorite pet died, she would be sure to have bigger existential concerns, about heaven and the afterlife.

I did not think through the theology back then. I just knew that getting her baptized was as important and crucial to me as getting her vaccinated. If there was a heaven, I wanted her to have an entry pass. At that point in my life, I had not really grappled with Catholicism, aside from coming to terms with my own unique Catholic belief system. I knew I was a feminist but could not predict that my feminism and faith would one day be on a collision course.

I figured I'd raise my daughter to be a liberal observant Catholic like me. While my Catholic beliefs were not entirely conventional, I could certainly give answers that were both comforting and progressively Catholic—silent on subjects I didn't have much time for—such as papal infallibility or the theory of original sin—and big on the social justice message of the gospels.

I did not foresee two developments: Valerie's refusal to conform to my predictions of her behavior, and the U.S. church's sharp turn away from the optimism and openness of Vatican II to a narrow, combative view of the world as something Catholics should shun. I also could not predict how misogyny, always a leitmotif in Catholicism, would soon infect the mindset of a new generation of Catholic leaders, particularly in the U.S.

From the very first, I should have known the "conversion" of my daughter was not going to be easy. We finally got around to baptizing her when she was eighteen months old. By then, my husband and I were living in Albany, New York. My parish church was welcoming, and I admired our pastor, who believed that Sunday sermons should last no more than seven minutes.

When I discussed baptism with him, the pastor was receptive. He seemed more struck by the fact that my spouse was Jewish than by his atheism. "Jesus was a Jew," he told me warmly. ("Yeah, Father, I've heard that one.")

The married deacon who baptized her agreed to omit the customary baptismal prayers for the father. The ceremony was a low-key affair, performed after Mass. My brother and mother were her godparents. She was wearing the sweet little white dress my uncle had sent as a gift.

The only reluctant party? Valerie. She forced the poor deacon to chase her all over the altar. It took about thirty minutes, but she finally was corralled and restrained, long enough to undergo the rite, performed at breakneck speed. I still have her baptismal candle, so I know it was legit.

I took Valerie to church every Sunday. We'd be in the sacristy with the other parents and children, watching—or trying to watch—Mass from the doorway. (This was before churches offered more hospitable spaces for families with small children.) My daughter's contribution? She taught the other kids how to tap dance on the marble steps.

When she grew older, Valerie expressed no curiosity about what was going on. When I received the host, she never begged to be included. When we attended a Mass that included First Communicants, I was so desperate I asked her if she wanted a white dress and veil like the other little girls. This was a child who insisted on wearing dresses to her day care center from the age of two. "No," she told me.

There was only one night when things were different. Valerie was upset, she'd been teased at school. I was trying to address her pain. I remember holding her hand and saying the Our Father out loud. I'm not even sure why. To comfort her? To comfort me? That same night, I made my routine long distance call to my mother. She did not answer the phone. I let it ring, ten, twenty times. My father finally came on the line. "I can't wake her," he told me. Two hours later, he called back. "We lost her," he said.

Valerie was my companion on that flight back to Rochester, New York, to attend my mom's funeral. (My spouse was out of town interviewing for a promising new job; I did not want him to miss his chance for a position we both hoped he would get.) She was with me at the funeral home, and at the funeral Mass. She never once asked me about her grandmother's future.

I never gave up. We ultimately moved to Northern Virginia, and I found myself in a parish that was far more conservative than the churches I had belonged to in the Northeast and Midwest. Despite my growing qualms about my Catholic faith, I continued to attend Mass, and she continued to attend with me.

By her teen years, it was clear that her Catholicism hadn't taken. After all, aside from baptism, she had not received any other sacrament. But I still wasn't worried. Or perhaps I just hadn't come to terms with my own daughter's religious skepticism. I really did not know what she thought. She was not the little girl I had been, someone who ran home from school and told her mother everything. I could barely persuade her to tell me anything.

Through high school and then college, I comforted myself with the thought that she believed in God and would find a path back to Catholicism, perhaps when she had children of her own.

And during these years, I was struggling with my own crisis of faith. I found Pope John Paul II and Pope Benedict XVI cold and judgmental. I winced when the Catholic bishops invested so much energy in restricting the reproductive rights of women. I considered myself a strong, professional woman whose views were respected in the workplace. But I had no such standing in my parish.

Like millions of other Catholics, I was disillusioned not only by the scandals of priestly pedophilia, but also by the church's attempts to cover up the abuse. I was appalled when the Leadership Conference of Women Religious was scolded by the Vatican for its "radical feminism," largely because the Sisters focused more on feeding the hungry and caring for the sick and vulnerable than on the bishops' bête noire—legal abortion.

I found myself wondering whether I could continue to be both a feminist and a practicing Catholic. I began a multiyear project interviewing progressive Catholic women and asking them how they addressed this conflict between faith and feminism. My project became a book, *Catholic Women Confront Their Church: Stories of Hurt and Hope.*

Pope Francis's election occurred as I was researching and writing the book, but Francis, who certainly has changed the tone of the church, still has done little to make it more welcoming to women. He's insisted that women cannot be ordained as priests, and he clings to the notion that a woman's true calling is motherhood.

The stories of the feminists I profiled both deepened and radicalized my Catholicism. I remain a Catholic, but on my own terms and with a conscience formed and matured by my encounters with these wise women, augmented by a lot of reading on church history and theology.

It wasn't until after the book was published that Valerie told me about her own faith journey. Actually, she didn't tell me. She wrote a blog post, explaining her atheism and how hard it was to reveal that to her mother.

It was only then that I learned that Valerie, as a child, had thought about God, had once drawn a picture of the divine with her pink marker as *a loosely human-shaped form made up of hearts.* She wrote that she had questions about religion, but never had raised them. She recalled a time in her life when she could appreciate the presence of God in the beauty and orderliness of nature.

But she had changed. *Somewhere along the line, during that progress into adulthood, I lost the ability to believe. I didn't want to stop believing, I just discovered one day that I didn't, like a switch had been flipped. I could still see all that beauty I had perceived in the world, but I could no longer see a pattern in its chaos.*

I think the realization that she had not shared any of her thoughts about God when she had faith hurt as much as the knowledge that those thoughts had vanished.

I never wanted her to be the "victim" of a Catholicism that devalues women and is obsessed with banning abortion, limiting contraception, and excluding LGBT Catholics from their faith. But I did hope she would ultimately see all the things I value about Catholicism—the liturgy, the sweeping poetry of the psalms, the message of the gospels, the sense that a divine presence permeates the world. My life is far richer because I'm a Catholic, even if tussling with my faith has given me a great deal of psychic pain.

I felt a sense of guilt and failure. Growing up, had she seen only the struggles, the feminist mother grappling with a sexist hierarchy that often enraged her? When we attended Mass, had she witnessed too much of my angst and too little of my joy? Had my growing disillusion with rigid Catholic orthodoxy made it easier for her to give up on any belief in God?

I am not worried about the state of her soul. Today, she is an activist, committed to the cause of racial justice, living out her values: someone I respect, admire, and love. Someone very much like her father. I just think it's far harder to live in an often cruel and unpredictable world without the anchor of faith.

However, growing up when she did—a generation removed from Vatican II—her "none-ness" may have been almost inevitable. We feminists raised our daughters to think for themselves, and to believe in their equality with men. How could we assume that they could countenance an institutional church that diverged so far from those values?

Over the course of writing my book, I met other Catholic feminist mothers. Five of the six adult daughters of the women I profiled no longer are practicing Catholics. It is not a comfortable state of affairs. But one we've learned to accept. As one of the mothers put it: "Some days I'm sad." But other days, she says, "I'm sorry. I just couldn't put that burden on them."

We can come to terms with our feelings. Our daughters will find their own coping mechanisms and sources of support. But the church? The church will lose its future.

Applying for Sainthood

Megan Merchant

My mother reached for the horse, to stroke the braided mane,
pet instead the electric fence. *Jesus Christ.*

This, I feared, all along, was her view of motherhood—tenderness
scraped from the bone.

She kissed a single dot of blood, pressed it to the ground.
Anima mundi.
Promised me a four-leaf clover would grow there.

//

I was never precious, but constantly ill. Each fever, a beatitude,
a prayer to the saint who fluttered the rafters.

Take her name, she said, when age came & I had to attach
my spirit to the church. I picked Elizabeth. She didn't last long.

//

When the animals fell, it became Francis. We dug trenches
for each damaged calf, each swatted bird.
Plowed the forty acres with sweat.

A woman's work,
I was taught, was to endure.

//

As her sight slipped, it became Helen,
who sustained on holy bread.

Helen of bones & hollows that would
scare the ravens from the roof, looking already dead.

My mother covered the horses' eyes with a veil.

//

Near the end, she moved to the foot of a mountain,
yoked complaints to the wind.

I still see her out at night,
racking up her list of curses, a fly swatter in hand,

in case that mountain tries to fling them back.
A woman must remain pure.

//

Hail Mary, body winged with claws,
my husband is concerned because he hasn't heard my cry.

I have been perched by the skunk-body
along the side of the road, slinging a pocket of colored
glass at vultures, to learn how death brings delight.

My mother never taught me her prayer for that—
how to rip it clean, how to boil the bones

and make a broth that sustains.

Mystic Trinities

Kelly Hedglin Bowen

A six-pound, nine-ounce bundle of original sin, I was doomed upon arrival. In my infantile state, I failed to realize the totality of my holy burden. According to the Catholics, I was responsible for the mistakes of Adam and Eve, people I'd never met. Until I was baptized, I risked an eternity in Limbo, and in my first wee weeks, I was forbidden to leave home. I didn't object when the priest doused my naked head with his sanctified holy water, making my miniature soul safe. I stayed sound asleep while his whispered prayers washed away my affliction. And just to be sure of my salvation, a tiny crystal rosary was hung around my neck, forever tethering me to an unseen God.

My mother was the driver of Catholicism in our family, raised up in a cult-like Irish faith that she dared not question. On Sundays, she dragged my sister Kristen and me to St. John the Baptist, where, from a Gothic jewel-encrusted altar that served more to intimidate than to enlighten, the Word of the Lord was preached down upon us. Like my mother, we were taught to revere the priests and their sermons, our devotion shown in our silence. Forced to sit up at attention on the hard wooden pews, we also learned to stand, kneel, and pray on cue. The Bible was an instruction manual—do this; don't do that.

There was no wiggle room for females in the Church. I was boxed in by generations of rote narrative about a woman's place before God and her husband. And truthfully, when I was young, I was excited by the prospect of my future as wife and mother.

I wore my first white lace veil on a sunny Mother's Day, when I made my first communion. With that sacrament, I was taught to share in the body and blood of Christ, to ingest His very essence, albeit in the form of a stale white wafer that clung to the roof of my mouth. His body entered my body, and, therefore, our bodies became one. Of course, the metaphysical message and the metaphorical cannibalism were beyond my seven-year-old comprehension; I was just thrilled to prance around the house as a baby bride-to-be.

I was indoctrinated in absolutes: the sole purpose of making love was for the conception that would create a pregnancy. My mom offered stern advice to her four daughters in sarcastic snippets: "Don't go out, procreate, and come home." As a young woman, I knew I was damned at every turn: damned if I had sex out of wedlock, damned if I used birth control to protect myself, damned if I became pregnant, and damned if I had an abortion.

I toed the Catholic party line through most of grade school, but by my teens, I had more questions than answers. At the mature age of fifteen, following my confirmation, the sacrament where I was made to promise that my belief and participation in Catholicism was of my own volition, I left the church. At the time, I failed to realize the mindset was already fixed.

~

Decades later, Harry and I, like all couples at the start of fertility treatments, were warned of the biological possibility of a multiple pregnancy. And, like most couples, we stayed focused on conception rather than what might come next. I imagine if every pregnant woman considered the multitude of known embryopathies—all the things that could go wrong—the human race would come to a screeching halt. To prepare my body to receive fertilized eggs, my beefed-up drug roster included Follistim and Repronex. Some evenings I shot three separate doses. I'd load the syringe pen with a glass vial of medication, similar to placing an ink cartridge in a writing instrument, screw on a disposable needle, and dial the correct dose. I'd pinch together a chunk of belly or butt skin and insert the tip of the pen into my flesh, slowly squeezing the injection button on the cap to release the hormone into my bloodstream. Thanks to my fatty tissue, the injection was virtually painless. For better and worse, motherhood has an addictive pull. I just closed my eyes and injected.

At the end of the cycle, to minimize our risk of multiples we took a conservative approach. Based on our doctor's advice, for my in vitro fertilization we replaced only three blastocysts back into my uterus.

Two weeks after my embryo transfer, I learned I was pregnant via a standard blood test. I was still giddy from the successful implantation when, at the week-five visit, following my first transvaginal ultrasound, the doctor announced twins. We privately celebrated our miraculous news for a week. Having twins was like hitting the fertility lottery—two for one and no more injections. The week-six ultrasound was supposed to be a follow-up, to check in on the twins' progress. But to our shock, we had *really* hit the fertility lottery: I was actually pregnant with triplets.

"Let me tell you how rare this is," the doctor said, as we sat huddled together, studying the ultrasound photos. Two of the three blastocysts had embedded, and then one of them had split naturally, into identical twins. "I recall only one case of mixed triplets prior to yours," he added.

I couldn't be sure whether he was trying to give us a warning or make us feel special. I stared at the film, trying to identify this new form. White strata blurred across a gray sky. Two black holes stared back at me. In the void on the right, I detected the faint outline of a single bubble. Taking a deep breath, I let my sight sweep over the screen, and as my eyes adjusted to the dark pool on the left, two distinct circles slowly surfaced.

"Triplets," I exhaled. After so much trying, a pregnancy was hard enough to believe—but triplets? I scrutinized the picture for an impression, a hint, something to confirm that what I'd seen was not an optical illusion.

~

In the days following that appointment, Harry and I bickered in hushed tones, as if our unborn children could hear us. Driving in the car, or standing in the kitchen stacking plates, we'd start into it again. I was trying to figure out the logistics of caring for three infants, while the thought of three itself and the finances bogged down my husband. Harry's linear approach to reason collided with my wider view of our future, and I resented him for it.

"Let's take this slowly," he would say, trying his best to maintain control.

We can't take this slowly! It's happening now—I have triplets. This instant, they are feeding off my body, drinking my worry. My blood screams through microscopic filaments, and in my veins, I feel the chill as three tiny heartbeats echo back.

I didn't say any of this out loud, of course—why panic my husband further?

A week later, we were sent to see a perinatologist, an obstetrician who specializes in high-risk pregnancies. As the technician slid the slick paddle across my bare belly, his hand turned in delicate circles, trying to capture an image for the screen. After a few silent pirouettes, he clicked off the machine, and the exam room went dark.

"If you wouldn't mind staying put," he said, "the doctor likes to review the images before you get up, in case he needs to check something again."

Harry stood next to me, his hand spread flat on my shimmering belly. "How do you feel?" he asked when we were alone.

"Sticky."

The door cracked open, and a fluorescent shaft of light split the darkness. I squinted my eyes to the glow. As if stepping onto a movie set, a white-coated man emerged, his voice beaming. "Kelly, Harry—a pleasure to meet you." He leaned toward me, as if I were an eager fan, and extended his hand. "We're all set here. Let's meet in my office. It'll be more comfortable to talk there—I'm about to tell you guys some things that are gonna scare the heck out of you."

~

The office was a small meeting room with a round maple table and a few cushioned chairs. Harry and I pulled together as close as possible—arms entwined as we braced ourselves for our lecture. We were alone for only a few minutes before the doctor joined us.

Dr. Libron[1] was clean-shaven with dark brown eyes. His manner was friendly, almost easygoing, as he dropped his folder on the table to pull me out of my chair and embrace me. His hug was full-bodied, familiar, the way some fathers might hug their daughters. But my father had never hugged me like that, so I was a bit shocked at his immediate tenderness. I came to believe it was Dr. Libron's way of giving me his physical support, letting me know I could lean on him, even before I realized I had to.

As he explained the wonder of embryogenesis happening inside my body, I realized that the creation story I learned when growing up left out the vital details. In sac A, I had seven-week-old monochorionic diamniotic (MoDi) identical twins. My embryo had split late following fertilization, resulting in their shared placenta, and it would be better if each of the babies had its own placenta—I think I heard this. Already, we spoke of the twins as a unique entity, a pregnancy unto themselves. In effect, they were.

On the other side of my womb was sac B, with my fat, happy eight-week-old singleton. With his own placenta, in his own space, he was developing blissfully, unaware of his complicated siblings falling behind in their development.

"I'm concerned about the lag time in gestational age," Dr. Libron said. "A shared placenta presents certain risks for a disproportionate blood supply." He explained that my pregnancy was in danger of twin-to-twin transfusion syndrome (TTTS), in which the twins' circulatory systems could fuse together as they developed. "There are specialists . . . prenatal surgery."

I drifted in and out of the conversation, grasping at threads of the discussion. I tried to take notes. But the words were heavy and awkward. There was no effective way for me to stay wholly present and absorb the magnitude of what was being explained—a shared placenta and neonatal surgery and selective reduction, never mind the likelihood of miscarried babies. I understood that he was talking about my body, but this wasn't supposed to be my pregnancy experience.

Just look out the window, I urged myself, studying the kernel-like buds on the cherry tree across the lawn. Harry pressed my hand if I seemed to be gone for too long, or perhaps he was holding on for dear life.

At that moment, I couldn't comprehend the abnormal characteristics of my triplet pregnancy. All I heard was that the twins would most likely die.

"Go home. Think about your options. You have time to decide your next steps."

Harry gripped me under my arm and steered me toward the door. I made it halfway to the parking lot before my legs buckled, and I slid straight down onto the sidewalk. My arms never left my sides to brace my fall. It was as though I'd collapsed from the inside out.

My faith had taught me that human life begins at conception. My religion had warned me that terminating a pregnancy is murder. As a single adult, I had tried to embrace my sexual independence and move away from this archaic and guilt-ridden dogma. I thought I had. But facing the microscopic reality of fetal development, I came to see those learned beliefs were as ingrained in my psyche as cellular division was rooted in my body.

To say my pregnancy was closely monitored would be an understatement; after the triplets presented, I had five separate doctor's appointments in four weeks. In the beginning, I'd foolishly assumed I had a typical age-related high-risk pregnancy, not realizing that I was part of an elite group. The .03 percent. Less than .03 percent of all pregnancies—fewer than three in one thousand—will result in MoDi mixed triplets. And of that number, a scant 7 percent develop TTTS. My twins had TTTS. I'd been too naive to know who Dr. Libron was or what a visit to his office meant when I was referred to him. As Chief of Staff of High Risk Maternal Fetal Medicine, Dr. Libron's specialty is a side of reproduction we don't often see: the thousands of women each year with high-risk pregnancies, and those couples who leave the maternity unit empty-handed.

I found no comfort when the doctor presented the various scenarios. It was possible—though, he emphasized, unlikely—that I could carry all three babies to term. I obsessed about a late-term miscarriage, envisioning fully identifiable body parts spilling from my womb, or a delivery that would last hours, only to end with my birthing three lifeless clumps.

If it were just the twins, my options would have been different. I could have opted for laser ablation surgery, a high-risk maneuver completed in utero. A laser would be used to sever knotted veins, tangled arteries, and other twisted bits and—the hope was—keep them independent. But it wasn't just the twins, so my choices for surgery and intervention after twelve weeks were limited. I could watch and wait and pray that the developmental damage to the twins was limited and sac B remained safe. But what if my healthy fetus in sac B was damaged during an invasive intrauterine surgery?

It was also likely that the twins, if they survived, would suffer life-threatening abnormalities; I was petrified by the lack of control I would have over my children once they left my body. (As if I had control of the pregnancy itself.) Could I knowingly and willfully give birth to biologically malformed infants, only to surrender them to a world where medical intervention would be their only means of existence?

And what about my singleton? How could I be a full-time, dutiful mother to his needs when my attention would understandably be focused on his siblings?

Then there was the inconceivable option. I could surgically drown the twins in their sac and try to keep the singleton. I had until the week-twelve mark to decide; if I elected to carry past the week-twelve mark and the pregnancy began to falter, fetal reduction would no longer be an option. Unable to discern the healthy fetus in sac B from the dying ones in sac A, my uterus would naturally and spontaneously abort the entire contents of the womb. The babies, as Dr. Libron put it, would go out with the bathwater.

I became fixated on my singleton, imagining my fat, happy bean suddenly ambushed by the unhealthy biological behavior of his siblings. When my body prepared to terminate, would he feel the rupture of being hastily torn from his tender nest? The sensation of pain as it stung his blossoming nervous system? I pictured his independent circulatory system, blood surging through his miniature veins, and then abruptly ceasing to flow as the blood tide shifted and washed him from my uterus.

Lost in a space where many women find themselves, I was haunted by these emotionally difficult questions—the ones few are willing to ask, though so many are quick to judge the women who dare. Who speaks to a woman about such things? Who warns her of the horrors of creation? Who listens when she needs to speak honestly about what is happening in her body? I deliberated over every aspect, stewed in it for weeks—mostly alone.

In my attempt to cull reputable medical research, I spent hours weeding through the politically and religiously motivated twaddle on the Internet. Frustratingly, there was little information to be found about TTTS. I dug for a definitive answer, seeking reassurance that my triplets could survive to term. But I did not uncover one personal report of a successful MoDi pregnancy with mixed triplets.

My therapist offered even less help. "Do you have a God whom you can ask to help you decide what to do?" she asked. But even after so many lapsed Catholic years, I knew my God's answer. Conception was at His hand, not mine. Who was I to engage in the forbidden practice of assisted reproductive technologies?

Despite the years I had been held hostage in the pew, my inner world was devoid of true spiritual guidance. My mother tried to offer what support she could about the triplets, but she lacked the words for the discussion. Her sorrow could be measured in silence and the miles between us. Whatever lay ahead—whether congenital disabilities or miscarriage or emotional suffering—was my cross to bear.

If it had been only the twins, I would have let biology take its course. But I had someone else to consider. It's a monstrous amount of pressure to place on a helpless fetus or an expectant mother: the burden of choice.

How does a mother choose? How does she decide to sacrifice the possibility of life for two embryos to enhance the chances of success for another?

She waits—day by day, hour by hour, minute by minute, up to the very last possible second. She talks to her awaiting souls, using her hands to communicate, sending tranquil circular currents into her dark womb. She spins a tale, telling them how much they are loved and wanted. She stares hard and long into the cloudy screen, begging for a sign. And then she asks them for guidance and permission and forgiveness.

At the heart of my final decision was how best to preserve my healthy embryo. And in the end, I chose life.

~

I trudged through those four weeks fueled by sorrow and exhaustion. In the long days between weekly ultrasounds, I cried constantly but willed myself to function. Each morning, I emphatically declared to the universe, *I am a mother of triplets!* I believed if I shouted it loud enough, maybe it would come true. But with each doctor's visit, it was increasingly clear that TTTS was developing.

"How are we doing?" Dr. Libron asked, when we returned to his office in week twelve.

"I'm going to hell," I answered. I wasn't sure if I actually believed this, but the guilt took its familiar place upon my shoulders so easily. I was going to hell one way or another, trying to fulfill my ultimate purpose and become a mother. IVF constitutes a mortal sin by the Church, never mind reducing implanted embryos even if they are unfit for life.

But with my decision made, I focused on doing what needed to be done for my child.

The scene never leaves me. Even as I write this today, I feel as if it is happening at this moment.

I am on my back on the hard exam table. Again. Smith, the technician, has the ultrasound paddle firm on my abdomen. His eyes do not have their usual brightness, and he is not as chatty. He lost his mother this week. I know this because he's scanned me so frequently. Despite his bereavement, he insists on being here, to see us through this part of our journey. I am thankful for his support and his skilled hand. Smith is familiar with my body, my triplets. He knows their development. An accurate reading on the ultrasound monitor is vital to the safe outcome of my pregnancy. Smith's scan will guide the hand of the surgeon through the reduction. And today, we will grieve together.

Harry assumes his usual post along my right side and places his arm around my head. I think he fears touching my stomach or getting in the way. On the monitor, three little beans present themselves together for the last time.

"Will you zoom in as close as possible?" I pray for a last-minute clue that might change the prognosis. I watch the image of sac A enlarge. Two microscopic bubbles floating in one black pool. The twins are bigger now, almost two inches in length, and the heads are discernable from the torsos. Little arm buds are present, and at high magnification, they almost resemble the rough sketches of the Peanuts character Schroeder hunched over his piano, except lying down.

My untrained eyes search every millimeter of the frame for hope. But what does hope look like? If anything, this last look confirms what I have been told. One of the twins is visibly lagging in size behind the other. A stuck twin—that was the actual phrase the doctor used. It is as if she were shrinking, her partner becoming the obvious dominant of the pair. It is not the evidence I want, but it is an omen I will not ignore.

"Ready when you are," Dr. Libron says.

I nod, and Harry kisses my cheek.

I am not afraid, even when I see the length of the syringe that Dr. Libron holds in his hand. Needles no longer scare me. The puncture is smooth, like a hot knife slicing through butter. The syringe piercing through my abdominal wall and deep into the uterine cavity feels as if someone is jabbing a finger into my belly. I am alert and attentive, my eyes fixed on the monitor. The procedure is mentally terrifying but physically painless. I watch the tip of the needle poke its way into sac A. The doctor's thumb presses his instrument, and a thin stream of potassium chloride floods into me. I am caught in the current as the liquid fills each tiny fetus and the pulsating lights of two fragile heartbeats cease.

I know to some people it is as if I held the precious heads of my newborns under their bathwater. I battle that vision myself, but then I remember that where faith offers hope, biology is merciless. I would have never been handed any swaddled infants.

The four of us watch silently as the doctor gently pulls the syringe from my belly. There is no bleeding.

"Everything went very well. I'm optimistic," says Dr. Libron.

Tears skirt sideways down my cheeks, a mixture of relief and panic. Now we wait. This is the hardest part of the procedure. We must wait eight minutes to confirm we still have a heartbeat in sac B. Harry cries, trying to hide his grief from me. We can be sad, I tell him. It is okay to be sad. Awkwardly, we hug each other. I am supposed to lie still.

The minutes pass. My abdomen is scanned a second time. I see Smith's grin before the doctor says a word. We have a heartbeat. We have a heartbeat in sac B. I exhale so deeply I am dizzy.

The weightlessness I feel as we walk back to our car surprises me. Today, the bright sky doesn't mock me, and I let the sunshine fill my face. For the first time in months, I'm not crying. I smile with relief.

"We are pregnant. We are going to have a baby," Harry says, and hugs me closer.

"Yes, we are," I answer, trying to believe him.

~

I'm mid-mascara at the bathroom vanity when my five-year-old peeks through the door and says, "Mom, imagine if there were three of me."

Carefully, I put the wand I'm holding back into its tube and stare in the mirror. "Excuse me?"

"What if there were three of me? Sometimes I think there are three of me," Deacon continues. Dressed in his racing car footie pajamas, he waits patiently for his answer.

"Then I would love all three of you," I say, kneeling before him and hugging him to me, "and you'd need a bigger room." I close my eyes and consider three Deacons running around my house, three pairs of rubber fireman boots lined up in the mudroom, three wet heads needing to be shampooed. He squirms as I hug him tighter, trying to squeeze the two other souls from his being.

~

My child was conceived by the skilled hand of an embryologist, under the watchful eye of a microscope. If our spiritual soul is a wholly separate entity from our earthly body, was this physically evident at my son's beginning? Why did Deacon's soul choose the one healthy body that embedded itself in me? What about the twins? Did their souls abandon their failing bodies before I intervened, or was there a celestial struggle for the lucky seat that reached its earthly destination? I am forever tethered to their unseen Spirits.

~

It's 2 a.m. when I hear Deacon call out from his bedroom. I wake so suddenly that by the time I get to his bedside, I'm chilled in a damp sweat.

"He's here, Mom," he says, eyes still shut tight.

"Who, baby? You're just dreaming." Bending down next to him, I gently kiss his brow. He's sleeping soundly.

"Someone that is in this family is not in this family."

"Sweetie, you're dreaming."

He opens his eyes wide, as if awake, and pushes himself up on his pillow. "No, Mom, someone that is in this family is not in this family."

"What happened, baby? Tell me."

"A dream I was having was ending, and someone called out to me, 'Hey!' It's real, and he's here. Here in my room. Someone said, 'Hey!' It's not in my dream."

"Was it a boy or a girl?"

"A boy—or maybe a girl. I couldn't tell."

"Did you say, 'Hey,' back?"

"No. I was scared."

"Don't be scared, baby. They just want to say hello." I kiss him again and smile.

I trace the outline of his face with the tip of my finger, following the gentle slope of his nose over his soft little lips and up under his chin. After a few minutes, the soothing motion relaxes him. On me, it has the opposite effect.

I'm often wide awake, searching for signs in the shadows. And sometimes, in my son's tender sleeping face, barely there—I catch a fleeting glimpse of the others.

Note

1. Not his real name.

My Mary

Adrienne Keller

An angel describes,
Passionately,
How great her son will be.
A teenager asks,
Sassily,
"Aren't you forgetting one thing—
I'm a virgin."
The church remembers?
Perfect submissiveness.

A small brown mother speaks
To her grown son,
Gives him THAT LOOK.
He sighs,
And takes care of the wine problem.
The church statues?
A tall silent lily white woman

An older woman
Stands erect and unmoving,
Defying Romans, Jews, and grief itself,

To watch her oldest son die a criminal.
The church honors?
A meek mild ever virgin.

The submissive girl?
No respect for her
The church statues?
No time for them
The meek mild ever virgin?
No need for her

Mary the impudent,
Mary the importunate,
Mary the brave,
She is my Mary.

Losing My Religion

Anita Cabrera

When my first son was baptized, I used the occasion as an excuse to get the family together. My siblings couldn't understand my foisting the Catholic upbringing imposed on us onto another generation and interpreted this as my being a reborn fanatic, suspicious that at any moment I might break out in stigmata. Granted, not one of my five siblings had children, and so had not been in the position themselves.

One sister flying in from the East Coast complained that the baptism date conflicted with an annual artichoke festival relatively close to where we live in California. She suggested we videotape the ceremony and she would watch it at a later time, so as not to miss the crowning of the Artichoke Queen or sample the more than one hundred artichoke-based culinary creations featured. "I don't believe in religion," she explained.

Neither do I, I didn't bother to clarify back.

Like many people raised with religion, I resisted it from the start. As a child, I disliked leaving the house Sunday mornings to sit still and quiet in straight-backed wooden pews for an eternity under our parents' admonishing glares if we whispered or fidgeted, the girls with heads covered, as protocol demanded, with little circular lace mantillas bobby-pinned to our heads like girly goyish kipahs, and my brother, dressed as a mini version of our father, in a tie and madras sports jacket.

A brief but exuberant foray into existentialism in my twenties, coupled with a discovery of Voltaire, Sartre, and Nietzsche, enhanced my disenchantment of organized religion. Besides, I had grown into a woman who better understood the feminist values picked up in a primarily female family that had long ago put down the Holy Bible for *Our Bodies Ourselves.* I could not abide the tenets of Western religion. None of these nonprofits for God, as far as I could see, lived up to the hype as a poster group for peace, love, and understanding. Apparently, in the name of religion, people waged wars, bombed buses, accepted bribes, and did unspeakable things to innocents all while preaching the damnation of the wicked before slipping off to party with them in cheap motel rooms. They laid claim to the worldly in the name of the Holy and, by definition, divided rather than united humankind.

But then I had children.

My husband, son of a Jewish, Holocaust-survivor mother and observant Greek Orthodox father, wanted nothing to do with religion. But I wanted to provide our child with *some* kind of spiritual footing and was willing to go in any direction.

"Just pick one," I told him. "And I'll join the team."

"I don't do religion," he reminded me, pointing out that Sunday mornings were reserved for the gym. "You handle it."

We live one block from a Catholic church and so I looked into having our son baptized.

Deacon Dan came to our house to discuss the baptism and asked my husband and me about own spiritual influences.

"What do you mean 'spiritual influences'?" Was he opening with a trick question?

"You know, what are your ideas about connecting with humanity or the Spirit?"

I answered unequivocally—the people in our Twelve-Step groups, the mainstay of my spiritual practices, a Group of Drunks, conveniently acronymized as GOD, making it easier for the religiously conflicted, including the spectrum of atheists and agnostics, to reconcile with the Higher Power concept central to the program's philosophy.

Smiling and nodding like a bobblehead doll, Deacon Dan spread his arms wide, as if inviting all those inebriates into his loving arms. “Great.” He told us to think of the baptism as our son’s introduction to the family of all human beings, including our spiritual mentors (and the wet drunks in the back row of folding chairs) from our Twelve-Step meetings.

So we started attending church.

Times had changed, or maybe we lucked out. The ambiance of the church near our house is far from funereal, most noticeable at its gatherings featuring Samoan dancers, mariachis, and an open bar. Some holy day Masses include Aztec dancers in loincloths, drumming and burning incense before the altar. On the Feast of St. Francis of Assisi, a priest leads a blessing of the animals on the sidewalk in front of the church, across from the bustling neighborhood cafe on the corner, and people of all faiths and none gather to have dogs, cats, rabbits, guinea pigs, lizards, birds, and even stuffed teddy bears blessed with holy water and prayers. My kids have assembled sandwiches after Mass for a food kitchen and delivered boxes of food and gifts at Thanksgiving, Easter, and Christmas to households needing the help, no matter the denomination or affiliation. Each December we make a pilgrimage, inviting anyone who can carry a tune or play an instrument, or not, to the St. Vincent de Paul Multi-Service Center near the freeway to sing carols for bag ladies, junkies, and the other down-and-out folks in need of shelter and a warm meal who clap and holler along. And when a neighborhood teen was shot dead, the church led a candlelight vigil through the streets, protesting the violence that had crept into our corner of the city.

Church no longer meant donning scratchy, ill-fitting dress clothes; the one thing I asked of my sons was to avoid items featuring celebrities or oversized brand logos. And to some, *that* would be a strict dress code. One contingent of parishioners who take church-chartered buses on gambling jaunts to Reno wear red satin baseball jackets printed up with their names on the back, taking them off only when approaching the lectern to read.

So when our youngest son Theo wanted to wear shorts to church, so be it. It was during a phase when he insisted on wearing shorts for about four hundred consecutive days, no matter the weather, except when outside on a trip to the mountains during a snowstorm. Even then, he wore shorts inside the lodge. Pants, he declared, were for losers, an ideology as unexplained as much of the Church's. He did make exceptions on occasion as a show of respect. When his cousin made her bat mitzvah, he wore black pants, black dress shirt, and a purple tie to match his brothers'. On Chanukah and Christmas when celebrating with relatives, Theo, again of his own volition, donned his formal dress outfit, asking for help only with the tie.

But compromise has its limits, and Theo announced he wasn't going to go through with his First Communion (*my* idea in the first place, he reminded me) if we allowed extended family to attend.

Understand: it's close to impossible to get our youngest to do things he doesn't want to. And before the childless childrearing experts weigh in, allow me to describe what it's like to take a six-year-old child to swimming class, wrestle him into a bathing suit, and throw him into the pool heated to ninety degrees (*for optimum comfort*). This is a kid who swam morning, noon, and night when on vacation near a pool. Yet, after three years of lessons, passing the swim tests at the various public pools, and feeling as if he had enough basic skills, he decided one day to go on strike and lie limp in the teacher's arms, refusing even to tread water to save himself. He would have let himself drown to not have to endure another swim class. When Theo announced he wasn't going to go through with the First Communion ceremony, I imagined the church version of the going-limp-in-the-pool strategy. We would dress him up, wrangle him into the pew and then, during Mass, when the choir paused and the priest invited the five little communicants up to the altar, the real show would begin.

Desperate for an accord, I tried a technique a child psychologist friend recommended: I listened to him. I sat at eye level with him and spoke in a softer voice than usual. "Theo, you've been doing so well; you've come this far. Why don't you want to finish? You've already memorized the prayers and your poem. Are you scared?"

Unable to hide his satisfaction at having learned the Lord's Prayer by heart, Theo in the recent weeks would recite it as fast as he could—Ourfatherwhoartinheavenhallowedbethyname—showboating his level of mastery. The children in Theo's group were given readings to choose from and Theo chose the plainest, a short poem thanking God for friends and asking help in being one. The kids had decorated felt banners to hang on the pews reserved for family members; Theo's featured stickers of Gogos, the latest collectible schoolyard fad; Pokémon cards; his own drawing of space warriors battling; two Lego constructions; and *Gaturro* and Lio comic strips—all things close to his heart.

"Are you afraid?" I asked, my head almost lying on the table as I looked up into his downturned scowling face.

Theo toyed with a "most wanted" Gogo, a stubby, sky-blue, one-eyed creature with a pointy nose, sliding it back and forth in front of him along our red Formica kitchen table. He kept his head down. "I'll do it, but I don't want anyone to see me." But his grandparents and cousin and aunt and uncle who all live nearby would want to see him, I explained. They'd be so proud of him.

"They can come if I don't have to wear pants. I don't want them to see me in pants."

It had taken bribing, extolling, and stern warnings to make it that far—we were discussing *what to wear* to the First Communion, way beyond *if* he'd make it. We'd temporarily switched congregations to attend one where Theo had friends in the same catechism class, coordinating things so that one of Theo's older brothers and *his* best friend enrolled at the same time for teen Confirmation classes, and going for fruit smoothies each Sunday when class was over. I had wanted to slip this religious education into the schedule in a seamless, natural way, and while it was anything *but*, it was happening. Why should a little detail like the length of one's pants get between a boy and his God?

And so I promised him he could wear shorts. What difference would it make?

If omission can be a sin, then I was guilty, at least in the sense of parental unity. I did not mention the agreement to my religion-disdaining but convention-adhering husband. Maybe it was partly deliberate, me flexing my theological muscles as the boys' religious education had been a duty I had taken on alone. Maybe I just wanted to avoid an argument.

On the morning of Theo's First Communion, after getting up early to prepare for a family brunch following the ceremony, I got Theo ready and dressed quickly. Theo's brothers and I were in the car waiting. My husband came out of the house, got in the car, slapped his hands on his thighs and huffed.

"Where's Theo? We'll be late."

"You talk to him. He wants to wear shorts." It was only then that I told him of the deal I'd struck with our youngest.

"Thanks for talking with me about it." My husband's face said it clearly; he'd felt edged out, I got it.

"I didn't think you'd care. What does it matter?" This was not the time to lay out my justifications.

"It won't kill him *not* to wear shorts one day," my husband countered. We'd been to enough couples' counseling sessions for me to recognize an underlying emotional dynamic that could veer us off course. My mistake was in making a pact with my kid without letting my parenting co-captain in on the decision.

Theo was sitting cross-legged in his closet crying when I found him. My heart broke; this was exactly what religious education isn't supposed to be about. "I'm not going to the stupid communion. I don't care."

I practiced getting down on his level and lowering my voice. "Theo, look. I don't care what you wear. God doesn't care what you wear. But your dad cares."

"And it's stupid."

"Totally," this time sounding as outraged and pissed off as he was. "You know what they say in AA? That you can have any God that you want. That no one else can tell you what God is or isn't; it's up to you. If you want to have a skater dude God who says F*** it! and doesn't give a damn about pants or shorts, you can. But your dad loves you and he would really be happy if you wore pants today. We can bring shorts and you can change right after Mass."

Theo stood up and put on some skinny jeans. He wore a hand-me-down plaid shirt with skateboard legend Tony Hawk's name embroidered in small lettering over the breast pocket and lime green skateboard shoes. He manned up and got in the car. During Mass, with his Greek Orthodox, Jewish, Catholic, and agnostic family members present, Theo explained what the wine symbolized when the priest put questions to the communicants; read his poem clearly, slowly, with a projected voice from the lectern; and took his first communion, which he and I agreed tastes sort of like the flying saucer-shaped wafers filled with tiny hard candies, only not as sweet.

Am I raising my children to be hypocrites, or worse, forcing them to go through religious rites only because it was *my* culture? I used to explain that I just wanted to make sure our kids would be able to catch Biblical symbolism in literature and references in pop culture, especially song lyrics and *New Yorker* cartoons. And it wasn't completely untrue.

Sitting in a garage won't make you Chevrolet: it's part of a popular adage in Twelve-Step programs. Another version would be *Sitting in church won't make you . . .* What? *Religious? Christian?* Yes, I was raised loosely Catholic, but I don't identify myself as Christian per se, regardless of doctrine. It's a loaded term implying convictions that are not mine.

But maybe sitting in church does do something.

Despite my penchant for going to confession in my first year of college armed with arguments picked up in Philosophy of Religion *just* to confront the darkened silhouette behind the confessional screen, sitting in church has given me something. I have felt soothed simply by passing an hour reserved for contemplation of a spiritual or metaphysical plane, a universal entity, one I envisioned, during my early days in recovery, as a saucy, gum-smacking, heavily made-up bleached blonde named Gloria looking down on us all. (After all, I was encouraged to believe in Higher Power of *my* understanding.) Or an hour to contemplate nothingness.

I am prepared for my children to someday reject the Church, argue the validity (or banality) of the Bible, decry the sins of a patriarchal hierarchy that has for centuries visited atrocities on the very people it preached to and systematically concealed and therefore abetted heinous crimes in its shroud of Papal saintliness. It seems only natural. Even Mother Teresa had her doubts.

But maybe my sons will find solace in something intangible when everything else seems to go to shit, as life sometimes does. When people, places, plans, and politics—the natural and material world—are not enough, maybe they will be open to a sublime connection with the universe that makes them feel less untethered or despairing. Or even hopeful.

A few weeks after Theo's First Communion, our family was invited to a bar mitzvah. Theo was also invited to his best friend's birthday party at a waterpark that same day. I gave him the choice, as it was his older brother's friend making the bar mitzvah. We would understand if he wanted to go to the waterslides. "It's a once-in-a-lifetime occasion," I said.

"A bar mitzvah is a once-in-a-lifetime occasion, too," Theo, in his seven-year-old wisdom, pointed out.

The bar mitzvah ceremony took place in an uncle's backyard in the Los Altos hills. A pool party would follow. I didn't ask Theo to dress up and was surprised when he put on long pants and a collared shirt. My sons sat attentively in the sun-drenched yard during the ceremony that lasted more than two hours. When it was over, the kids jumped up and screamed, scrambling after candy thrown at the crowd, stuffing their pockets full of Tootsie Rolls, Starbursts, and Warheads. As the luncheon reception wound down, I was ready to leave but offered to stay longer as Theo was still playing with the other younger siblings.

"No; I'm tired." More teenagers were arriving and more adults leaving as we said our goodbyes and headed back to San Francisco, leaving his brother to come home hours later with some friends. "Can I watch SpongeBob when we get home?"

"Sure," I said, expecting he'd be out by the time the San Francisco fog enveloped us. I glanced at him from time to time in the rearview mirror and finally saw him lay his head against the back seat, eyes closed. "I should have worn shorts," he reflected.

The Enunciation

Devin E. Kuhn

Mary Mary, Quite Constrained,
How does your garden grow?
From the loom of your womb
A boy god is groomed

And blessed is that fruit
But you are doomed
to remain forever mute.

**MARY IS QUEEN BY GRACE BY KINSHIP
BY CONQUEST
BY CHOICE OF GOD[1]**

What choice had she
A young bride-to-be

When god got her pregnant
And no Planned Parenthood for centuries

Weaving her own world
When Gabriel leaped through the window
To deliver the staggering blow
Mary Queen by Conquest
Was forced to consent, no chance to say no

MARY IS MORE MOTHER THAN QUEEN[2]

And should anyone venerate her
or for a goddess mistake her,
We'll have it known
She's a mother, a virgin,
An incubator
Not someone fit for a throne

Virgin with child
Mother without sex

The woman women
emulate
may be
impossible
but certainly
not
royalty

THERE IS NO STAIN IN YOU O MARY[3]

Mary
unmarked, unstained
restrained

Does not bear the burden:
wanton
wanted
woman

Thou Art
Serpent god
Giver of fruit
trading knowledge for babies
gardens for free will
Banishing from both

The Annunciation:
An Enunciation—
Renunciation or repudiation

VICTORIOUS ARE YOU HOLY VIRGIN MARY AND WORTHY OF ALL PRAISE YOU ARE THE VIRGIN WHO CRUSHED THE HEAD OF THE SERPENT[4]

TERRIBLE AS AN ARMY SET IN BATTLE ARRAY[6]

What would have happened
if Mary crushed
the head
of the
serpent,
the thrust of his will,
his divine word

Wrote her own story

Woman who was weaving

Stained by
this
Original Sin

Notes

The phrases noted here are inscriptions from the Basilica of the National Shrine of the Immaculate Conception in Washington, D.C.

1. The "Mary is Queen by grace . . ." quotation originates with Pius XII in his messages to Fatima, *Bendito seja* (*AAS* 38. 266).

2. "Mary is more mother than queen" is attributed to Saint Thérèse of Lisieux in *The Little Flower.*

3. "There is no stain in you, O Mary": Though phrasing varies, the concept of Mary born "without stain" is an accepted part of Catholic Catechism, codified by Pope Pius IX in 1854, and noted in the Legion of Mary prayers, and elsewhere.

4. Many Catholic sources associate Mary with the person described in Gen. 3:15 who will bruise or crush the serpent's head. In artwork, Mary is frequently portrayed with a serpent beneath her feet.

5. "Who is she that comes forth like the rising dawn, fair as the moon, bright as the sun, like the rainbow gleaming amid the luminous clouds, like the bloom of roses in the spring" is inscribed in the Chapel of Our Lady of Guadalupe in the National Shrine of the Immaculate Conception. This celebratory verse is a variation of the Song of Songs 6:10, which has been interpreted within Catholicism to refer to Mary.

6. Song of Songs 6:10 ends more powerfully than is suggested by the quotation in note 5, however. The NIV translation continues with "majestic as the stars in procession," while the KJV, ESV, and other translations end with variations of "majestic as an army with banners." The Antiphon to the Catena Legionis similarly interprets the ending of 6:10 as "terrible as an army set in battle array." These all allude to the strength, power, fierceness, and majesty of Mary that is often overlooked.

Magdalene

Jeannine Marie Pitas

I did not waver at the sight of him.
A beloved apostle, I clung to the wood of the cross,
refused to avert my eyes.

Where the mind dwells, there lives the treasure.
While the rest of you ran away and hid,
I, determined, waited.

Later, envious, you refused to believe
in my testament of the empty tomb,
my faith that our beloved walked again.

You did not stone me,
but sent me off
to speak with stones,

beauty rent with a thought
for the thrust of the sword,
a fat pope's word.

Five hundred years later, Gregory
called me a prostitute, or else the sister
of Lazarus, or maybe his mother.

My message is the same: Hell is no worse
than the world you are making
as you tune out the news that could have saved you

and tear the flowers out of the earth.
If you need me, I'll be in the place called barren
where my deathless beloved brings forth water

from rocks, transforms it into wine,
and I make treasures from my mind—
the truest promised land.

Those of you now known as prophets
will come, like me, to be known as sinners—
Like me, you'll speak of resurrection and not be believed.

My roots drag color from sand,
my rivulets flow with gold,
and you'll remember the beloved apostle.

But the desert is vaster than your mind can imagine.
So go on. I dare you.
Try and find me.

Transubstantiation

Maryanne Hannan

What we used to call the miraculous process
by which
"what stands under goes across."

What,
you say?

Imagine Father Dumb Ox
in his medieval glory rolling that one around.

The rest of us—not so much. Two prefixes,
two suffixes, and that tricky root, *sta*.

Sure, *trans*port, *sub*way, *sta*tionary
help, but light bulbs of recognition?
Sorry, Operation Dusty Darkness.

Until recently.

When *trans* slipped its prefix strait jacket,
became a noun, an adjective, and now
look—a verb. In fact,

there's a whole *trans* community
out there, insisting what stands under
must,
    does
        and will go across.

Our Hail Mary Pass

Devin E. Kuhn

A prayer from my mother
whispered each night
nestled among forehead kisses
before I slip off to sleep and stars

Warm breath
seeps into blood, into bone
and decades later,
after wrestling with the rough edges
of what Catholic means to a feminist

Catholicism calls me home,
familiar as family
the cool dark, the hard pew, the rituals and intonations
enfold like a womb
like coming home
the embrace of a parent
safe in their arms,
no matter how hard I push
to create my own space,
shape it as my own
negotiate revise
reveal

A prayer now for my daughter
whispered each night
nestled among forehead kisses
before she slips off to sleep and stars

Warm breath
seeping into blood, into bone
into her memories
her self

How do I enshrine this in her,
without burdening her
with only God the Father and Lord,

How do I show her
God as
Mother
midwife baker potter shepherd protector forgiver friend
God as
generous peaceful compassionate
God who is
both male and female
God who made us in her image
With both hands
I hold her up
That she may know
the strength
of centuries of women
with powers
like her own
to create
revise
envision
generate
to be
her full self
her godself

A prayer, mother to daughter:

Hail Mary
Full of Grace and Strength
The Divine is with thee
Blessed art thou
as are all women,
and blessed
is the fruit of our wombs, our minds, our hands:
Creation.
Holy Mary,
Mother of God,
Please pray
for us all,
Now,
and every hour
of our lives.
So be it.

Part Three

Spiritual Activism and Utopian Vision

Not Faith

Jillian Egan

I came to you a body full of rags
on feet of snapping cable
My mouth-sounds—too soft for gnashing
too sharp for languid prayer—
only added up to
hope
I am not overcome with tongues
I only praise in a prescriptive language
a word-set locked in time
a ritual bereft in the corner
a dunce cap up in arms over news
that girls could now serve
I came to you a sightseeing rosary
resting on a layman's thigh
craning for a peek in the inner rooms
to see for myself that you were not there—
that you could be anywhere
here
Return me to form
I'd have asked if I were wise
But where does it leave us
that I begged to be riven anew

I Could Have Been a Psalmist

Pat Brisson

I wish a woman had written the psalms.
I think there would be less:
Vent your wrath on them
and let your burning anger take hold of them
and more:
Oh, God, you are my God
for whom I have been searching earnestly.
My soul yearns for you
and my body thirsts for you,
like the earth when it is parched,
arid and without water.
And it goes on like that for eight more lines,
personal, emotional,
almost erotic but then
as if it's hitting too close to the bone
the psalmist switches back
to a violent image:
those who seek my life . . .
will be slain by the sword
and their flesh will become
food for jackals.
This is not to say that women

don't ever have violent tendencies,
but I think we're a lot less likely to write them down
and call it a prayer.

On Desire and Direction

Lindsey White

I believe Etty Hillesum was speaking about desire when she once wrote, "I don't want to be anything special. I only want to try and be true to that in me which seeks to fulfill its promise." I want, I desire the same thing for myself. To fulfill my own promise. I know this now after a long journey of arriving to it.

There's just one problem . . . I'm often very good at letting outside voices confuse and cloud my own.

I could not tell you why I wanted to speak to my own truth, only that I knew I should. And once I was asked to write on this topic, I laughed. Not because there's anything particularly funny about it, but because I felt like I was the least qualified person to speak about trusting God while following your own arrow.

I can speak freely as to what happens when you allow other things to get in the way of knowing and following your desires. That part is easy. The far more interesting question, and the far more difficult one, is what it costs to not follow or consider those desires at all. I was asked to write about how my own play into the course of my life. How intentions and prayers they're based in lead me to God. How they ultimately inform and direct my actions. My initial uncertainty revealed something important. Its very presence was exactly why I needed to accept this invitation.

At barely twenty-two, I was convinced I had the whole thing figured out. My desires pointed east, toward Washington, D.C., toward law school. I wanted to be the voice for the voiceless, an instrument of God's peace. I had an undergraduate degree from a Jesuit university. I was ready to set the world on fire. The catechism I received there wasn't just doctrinal, but practical. It included courses in critical race theory, weekly service hours at homeless shelters and detention centers, and liberation theology as our gospel. I wanted to continue. I was convinced that becoming an attorney would be the most perfect and selfless way to serve God's people, especially the marginalized.

I thought of myself and my future career path as *such* a gift.

They also say pride goeth before the fall, right?

How grateful was I that I managed to do all of this in a way that was both socially acceptable and that made my family so proud. As it turns out, I could have it all exactly the way I wanted. I would retain the privilege of joining the legal profession while still holding onto the moral integrity that comes with fighting for justice. The superiority I felt was extremely comforting. I was going to go out there and *do something that mattered.* I had no idea what it would be, but I knew it would mark me as a good person.

My desires, though well intentioned, were so disordered. I focused more on what I thought the world wanted of me, of the role I thought I should play, rather than what I wanted for myself.

And on the surface, I appeared to be performing as the person I wanted to be just fine. I joined lots of organizations with the words "human rights" in the titles. I kept up with the grind of classes, punishing myself appropriately for indulging in any moment I took to breathe, as was expected of me by law school culture.

I stopped caring about myself at all. Getting to the next accomplishment, and achieving it was the most important thing. The only thing that mattered.

I tried to cling to the role of the caretaker and crusader that I had created, but I was failing miserably. Because that's the thing about living only on the surface: once its fragility shatters, you often end up drowning in the depths below. It happened slowly, and with my deliberate choice not to look any closer at it, but I could no longer ignore the doubt that was now boiling over in the pot I thought I'd watched.

I stopped praying. It felt like God had gone silent too.

It was February 2016. The color had seeped out of my world. A coldness crept over my heart. Alone in the gray and scared as hell, I was drowning in my uncertainty and my doubt. And there seemed to be nothing to hold onto. Everything I loved, everything that made me feel like a person, seemed to be slipping through my fingers. I lost interest in the world outside my apartment. Any conversation with friends or family became a chore. I became uninterested in reading and writing, which have always been the great loves of my life. And most painfully, my spiritual life dried up. I remember lying on the floor of my apartment, holding my grandmother's rosary, tears of frustration streaming down my face. Pleading, begging, shouting at a God I felt so far away from for anything at all. Anything to fill the emptiness that was swallowing me whole.

Eventually, I stopped fighting for myself. I couldn't keep going. And the shame I felt, if that was true, how could I possibly believe that I could be of service to others at all?

I held tightly to fear. Submitted to it. I let it lead me, because it seemed to be the only truth I could understand or accept. But as I tumbled to the bottom, reaching out for help no longer became optional. I was caught by so many who love me. I know now that each conversation, every act of care or kind word from another person was a small grace that kept me going.

And a curious thing started to happen: They all began asking me, "What do you want?"

I couldn't come up with a single answer. And it stayed that way for longer than I care to admit.

Andrew Solomon once wrote that we *need* to embrace our sadness, because that sadness just might be the foundation from which we rebuild our lives. Accepting that is certainly a choice, and I suspect it's definitely not a one-size-fits-all piece of wisdom, but it was the first choice I made out of the hell of my worst major depressive episode. Embracing it mattered, because there was no going back for me.

It still matters, to this day.

Because I know God was a part of it.

I don't remember the hour or the moment, but something broke through the mold that coated my soul. And I wanted again. I wanted more, and better for myself. And I set out to relearn who I am on the other side of all that darkness.

I desired.

I would like the story to have a neat way of wrapping up. I would like to say I never had another moment of doubt because I had a serious Come-To-Jesus moment. I would like to say I can see myself as one of the lilies in the field, and that I am filled with peace and a wondrous sense of God's love. And I would *love* to say I have tangible, concrete, easily explained desires. I don't. They're not career goals, or specific achievements. I can't talk about them as though they exist in a five-year plan, nor will they be accomplished in any other neatly set timeline.

I would really like to say I let go of my fear easily because it no longer served me. I haven't. Not completely, because, in truth, holding onto fear can be comfortable.

But as an old friend and spiritual director once told me, fear makes for a poor leader. Do not use it as your guide.

In the past five years, I have done *so many* things afraid. I have been absolutely terrified, but I have done them anyway. I've decided to try faith—in all of its unknowability, in all of its mystery—instead. It's taught me how to walk through that fire.

Not long after a formal diagnosis and an attempt at medication management, I sat in a field across a narrow blacktop highway that runs through the Blue Ridge Mountains. I made a promise to myself and to God. I called it a covenant because the word itself encompasses both a relationship and an agreement. I want to believe it put some real weight behind my prayers, just as it once did for the Israelites. I began to see myself again as another of God's lost but well-loved children. I tried to keep the terms as simple as I could: "I will follow where you lead, if you will help me find my way to you. But you must hold my hand. Help me find my way home." Letting go of what's destructive—doubt, fear, uncertainty—is scary. But there's a freedom on the other side that left me wanting more. There's a trust that God and I have started to repair.

And I know there's a reason Jesus told the disciples to leave everything behind them on the journey. I doubt he meant only material possessions.

It's been a slow process of unlearning and relearning. I've scraped the rust off some of the desires I've had for quite a while. I still want to fight the good fight, and that's needed in this world now more than ever. But I don't know where it will take me, or what it may ask of me. I know I need to belong to a community that accepts and respects me. I'm lucky enough to have found that. I have never been asked to make myself smaller within my parish. After years of being shamed into silence, the freedom to speak and be heard is life-giving.

I've cultivated new desires that expand my horizons. My hunger for silence surprises and comforts me. The space in my heart for those struggling with mental illness continues to grow. And after many painful months of not being able to sit down in front of a blank page, I've finally returned to writing, especially writing as prayer, a practice I've honed since childhood.

There's a prayer from Thomas Merton that I return to often. I'm sure many in my position in life have drawn comfort from it.

My Lord God,
I have no idea where I am going.
I do not see the road ahead of me.
I cannot know for certain where it will end.
Nor do I really know myself,
And the fact that I think I am following your will
Does not mean that I am actually doing so.
But I believe that the desire to please you
Does in fact please you.
And I hope I have that desire in all that I am doing.
I hope that I will never do anything apart from that desire.
And I know that if I do this, you will lead me by the right road,
Though I may know nothing about it.
Therefore will I trust you always, though

I may seem to be lost in the shadow of death.
I will not fear, for you are ever with me,
And you will never leave me to face my perils alone.[1]

Faith can so often feel like journeying. The long and short of it is this—we ache for what feels like home. For wholeness, acceptance, peace, and belonging. We hunger for the place where we can embrace who we truly are, without apology, without compromise. The place where we shine, together.

And what might I desire? The ability to soak fully in God's love. To live in the holy silence of my heart, where God whispers gently. To love kindness, act justly, and walk humbly with my God at my side.

To determine my own part in building God's kingdom.

All journeys have destinations, and they are the full expression of who we are, but it is the middle space itself where life takes place. This is where I'm lucky enough to be caught now. To be sure, I have moments where I stumble. Where the road is uncertain, and my steps get heavier. But in spite of all this, I know I'll carry on. The bad days no longer outnumber the good, and those moments of goodness are so sweet. More often than not, they melt away into joy.

It is no longer difficult to find God in all things, in all places. And because I am beginning to know myself, I have begun to know my true desires. It's getting easier to find and follow the signposts on my way.

The latest one? To go back to that holy mountain place, renew my covenant to myself and my God. And continue to walk with my chin up, into whatever may come. I have truths that need speaking, wants, hopes, and dreams—I hold them close to my heart in a wider world and a church that fears a woman who uses her voice. One that cannot be smothered or silenced, not when God speaks in me and through me. Unruly and Catholic, untamed and apostolic. I am named as beloved daughter. My desires put the courage behind my convictions. I am ready to follow where they lead me.

It is the unavoidable adventure, the faith and the fellowship we carry along that make up the beauty and purpose of any soul's journey. And I truly believe the path itself is created out of want and hope, bringing us closer to God. Our desires, our deepest truths, can serve as cardinal directions if we are brave enough to let them guide us.

Note

1. *Thoughts in Solitude* (New York: Farrar, Straus, Giroux, 1956), 79.

The Heretic

C. R. Resetarits

The Heretic in lieu of Easter Mass sips blood-orange mimosas
on the weathered deck of a rented house on Folly Beach.
She floats in the briny arms of rolling waves, a child again.

The Heretic ponders Marys, Christs, and Popes but only dolphins
past the breakers make her smile, only the sun bleaches
bone-snow white her inclinations. Sun/salt basted,
she ponders knots of seaweed crisscrossing her feet.

The Heretic chases grace alone. Her own heart plumbs
the disquisitive depths of the ocean's salt-sanctioned breeze
or opposing muck-riddled marsh. The Heretic stays derelict

but not in jest nor in a state gone slave or posed but in a state
less safe than circum-pomp or circumstance. Her blessing/blame
a sun-kissed soul, her penance dancing in between the diadem
of priest or king, that hat of thorns, the head of pins.

Unfinished

(upon the completion of a doctorate of ministry)

Marci Madary

I am a lay woman,
married, widowed, single and married again.
White, cis-gender, and straight.
Middle-aged, student and searcher.

I am a questioner and subtle disturber of the peace.
Consistently Catholic yet
unsettled in my pew:
faithful to a greater God.

I am a theologian and a minister
in a church that is blind to my vocation,
a scholar with the wrong initials,
a pastor devoid of a congregation.

I climbed a mountain,
scaled an icy headwall,
only to be forced to forge a new path
in a land not my own.

Adolescent questions
have circled back around:
where do I fit in this world
during another time of transition?

Perhaps my place is not fitting,
being outside the walls
with the many who abide there,
missing the shelter but not obligated to conform.

Perhaps the only true answer
is another question.

La Llorona

Jeannine Marie Pitas

I am not la Virgen de Guadalupe, that praying goddess
in blue and pink, cocooned by spikes, a yellow fence.
For hours I knelt before her image, asked her what
made her demand a church built in her name.
She pretends to give without taking—she hears our prayers
and stands on them like those roses beneath her feet,
lets our cancer and heartbreak and unpaid bills adorn her.
I tried to live in such unlaughing, unweeping compassion,
a love that pretends to ask nothing from no one.

I am not la Malinche, the conquistador's interpreter,
America's original Eve. In the painting she rides
with Cortés on his horse, every little girl's fantasy
of growing up beautiful, desired, loved, not knowing
that so often they'll end up *chingada,* remade into an instrument
for the use of some man. I wonder how she felt as her people's
temples were looted, women and children enslaved, thousands
of years of history erased. I too have painted futures
from the blue, green, brown watercolors
of men's eyes, crystal palaces from their light.
But really I have nothing a conquistador would take.

Instead, I want to be la Llorona, that weeping mother who,
enraged, drowned her children to spite the man
who betrayed her. Like her I walk the earth, struggling
to believe I'll find them, not accepting I've drowned
the beloved future that came out of me.
La Virgen stares down in compassionate reproach,
La Malinche looks up and laughs,
I walk and walk with my graveyard flowers,
begging the singer to give me mercy, hoping
one day I'll return to heaven
and find a door ajar.

The Lydian Woman Speaks to the Dead Saint

Becky Gould Gibson

> There is neither Jew nor Greek, there is neither bond nor free, there is neither male nor female: for you are all one in Christ Jesus.
>
> —Galatians 3:28

No longer on your travels,
you've taken up residence
in chapter and verse,
your words on the tongues
of men and women,
your words no longer your own.
Come in by the fire.
You welcomed us. You did.
You said you heard
Jesus in the road.
Did you beget your own savior?
New promise.
New creation.
When if ever do we stop waiting?

The Church failed you.
Phoebe you called deacon.
Junia you called foremost
among the apostles—
Junia/Junias/Junia—
named and unnamed sisters
tossed on the bone-heap.
Had Jesus been a woman,
not God's son
but God's daughter,
would you have preached her?
Cramp in the belly,
pain in the side—
not once and it's over,
sacrifice done,
but once every moon
death sheds its skin.
Would you have deemed
her blood glorious,
childing a worthy sacrifice?

Summer Solstice

Teresa Delgado

All creation reveres the moment
    When sun arches to its highest place
    When earth is bathed in warmth
    And the lion lies down with the lamb.

Tranquil dawn defies the astronomical event
    of sun's proximity to longing earth
    of fire signs sparking, reigniting
    of red phoenix laughing,
        heart pulsing dangerously close to catching fire.

Ancient divinity rests between pyramids of old
    touching transcendence but for a time
        long enough to generate star systems anew
    embers still burning in midsummer night sky
        streaming southward in a trail of crimson light.

By daybreak, all recedes

Moment passing in an instant dream
    To begin the long journey yet again
        Farther from reach
            from touch,
                from warmth's gaze
                    yearning immanence.

Earth and sun perform their revolution
    When space intervenes to claim its due
    With a promise to resume the dance
    In what seems an eternity.

All creatures revel in the moment
    Of sun's arc at its highest place
    Creation made to stand in wonder
    And lion lies down with lamb.

    All is peace
    All is fire
    All is new
    All is one.

Summer solstice

As I reflect on my poem "Summer Solstice"—its inspiration, its content, the occasion for its writing—I am struck by how the embodiment of my feminist—that is my Latina womanist—sensibilities are operative. For one, I am a theologian by vocation and yet, as I learned firsthand from my dear mentor and advisor, the trailblazing womanist theologian Delores S. Williams, I must never lose the capacity for poetry, for capturing beauty, agony, delight, and wonder in words that pierce. Through her guidance, I learned the lesson of the "both/and": to embrace the multiple attributes of my identity even when theological language and spaces, including the church, could not—as mother, activist, theologian, poet, dancer, teacher, lover. It is a product of feminism's third wave: an affirmation that we, as women, hold in our very bodies the multiplicity of crossroads that cannot, and must not, be defined by anyone but ourselves.

Similarly, the pattern of the summer solstice—its anticipation, its moment of intensity, its departure and return—provides a reminder, and perhaps a corrective, against the false expectations that the struggle for equality, inclusion, and equity is completed once a particular battle is won. All movements for justice have their respective ebb and flow, of alignment and retreat. This most recent feminist wave of intersectionality is challenging us with new language, but it is part of the same pattern; #MeToo is but a manifestation of the same struggle, in a different context and with new voices. As waves demonstrate, this movement of fourth-wave feminism has come crashing against the shore in similar force and impact as the others. The intensity and magnitude of the ocean of voices around it will contribute to its ability to erode the sexist/racist/misogynist/classist/homophobic structures that it will meet upon impact. As waves, this movement too will eventually retreat, and the waters will take on the appearance of calm for a time. This poem is a reflection of my enduring hope for all who live on the margins of our society, including of our church, that as long as injustice exists with a force as strong as gravity, there is always the possibility that the brightest, warmest and most intense light will make its way around again.

She Will Rise

Lizzie Sextro

She will rise,
not because you have risen her, but
because her toes will burrow into the cool dirt
and she will plant her feet into the earth,
and water her roots with lament.

She will rise,
not because you offer your hand, but
because the scars on her palms from playground
bullies have taught her legs that
they are stronger than the fall.

She will rise.
Her hips will house kin-doms and her
womb will birth light. She will shine
when she stands and when she stands, she will
invite Mary Magdalenes to join her.

She will rise:
Her vocal chords will expand until her song
bursts forth with brave vibrato. In the name of
mothers, she will rewrite parables to match
their harmonies.

She will rise, rise, rise.
She will resurrect stories from abandoned
graves until they reach lips and tongues. She will
find dirt under her fingernails from digging
and drink the lost words of our foremothers.

Notes on Contributors

Kelly Hedglin Bowen is a writer, activist, and sailing instructor. She teaches creative writing from her floating classroom on Lake Champlain. A passionate and vocal advocate for women and reproductive health, she writes to expose the underbelly of the motherhood myth. Before finding her way to the page, Kelly was a Global Trade Director focusing on business development and foreign affairs. She is fluent in Russian. Her prose appears in *Creative Nonfiction*, *The Fiction Advocate*, *The Pitkin Review*, *VT Digger*, *The Burlington Free Press*, and *The Huffington Post*. Her essays have been shortlisted for the 49th Annie Dillard Award for Creative Nonfiction, the Creative Nonfiction Dangerous Creations Prize, the 2017 Arts & Letters Prize in Creative Nonfiction, the Under the Gum Tree (dis)Empowerment Contest, and the New South Prize. She holds an MFA from Goddard College. Her essay included here is taken from a chapter of her in-progress memoir *Mystic Trinities*.

Pat Brisson writes books for children and poetry for adults. Her picture book, *The Summer My Father Was Ten*, won the Christopher Award in 1998. Her poem, "The Cleverness of Seeds," was an honorable mention in the Thomas Merton Poetry of the Sacred contest. Other poems have appeared in *The Paterson Literary Review*, *The Edison Literary Review*, and *The Journal of the Society of Classical Poets*. She has won the New Jersey Governor's Volunteer Award for her work with Project Storybook, helping incarcerated women choose and record books to send home to their children.

She volunteers weekly at the Catholic Charities Food Pantry in her town. She and her husband have four grown sons; they live in Phillipsburg, New Jersey.

Anita Cabrera writes short fiction, poetry, and creative nonfiction that explore the themes of addiction, mental illness, and the complex nuances in parent-child relationships and marriage. Her work has appeared in *The Berkeley Fiction Review*, *The Berkeley Poetry Review*, *Brain, Child Magazine*, *Colere*, *Acentos*, *MomEgg Review*, *The Ravensperch*, *Deronda Review*, and the *Squaw Valley Poetry Review*. She was the winner of *The New Guard's* Machigonne Fiction Award in 2017. Ms. Cabrera lives with her spouse and sons in San Francisco, California, where she teaches college writing classes with a focus on community engagement, dances, and rides bikes, but not necessarily in that order.

Dinorah Cortés-Vélez is associate professor of Spanish at Marquette University in Milwaukee, Wisconsin. She specializes in colonial and contemporary Latin American literatures and cultures. She has published one poetry chapbook and books of fiction. She has completed a manuscript for a scholarly book entitled *"Sin que a uno u otro se incline": La filosofía de género de Sor Juana Inés de la Cruz" ("Not to Either State Inclined": The Philosophy of Gender of Sor Juana Inés de la Cruz).*

Teresa Delgado is director of the Peace and Justice Studies Program and professor and chairperson of the Religious Studies Department at Iona College in New Rochelle, New York. Her publications include "Metaphor for Teaching: Good Teaching is Like Good Sex" in *Teaching Theology and Religion*, and "Beyond Procreativity: Heterosexuals Queering Marriage" in *Queer Christianities: Lived Religion in Transgressive Forms* (New York University Press, 2014). Her book, *A Puerto Rican Decolonial Theology: Prophesy Freedom*, was published in September 2017 (Palgrave Macmillan). She has served as president of the board of WESPAC (Westchester People's Action Coalition) and as a member of the board of trustees of

Colgate University. She lives in Mount Vernon, New York, with her husband, Pascal Kabemba, and she is the proud mother of their four beautiful children: Francesca, Celeste, Josiah, and Xavier.

Jeana DelRosso, PhD, is Sister Maura Eichner Endowed Professor of English, and professor of women's studies, at Notre Dame of Maryland University in Baltimore. She is the author of *Writing Catholic Women: Contemporary International Catholic Girlhood Narratives* (Palgrave MacMillan, 2005). She is co-editor with Leigh Eicke and Ana Kothe of *The Catholic Church and Unruly Women Writers: Critical Essays* (Palgrave MacMillan, 2007), *Unruly Catholic Women Writers: Creative Responses to Catholicism* (SUNY Press, 2013), and *Unruly Catholic Nuns: Sisters' Stories* (SUNY Press, 2017). Her articles have appeared in books as well as in such journals as *NWSA Journal*, *MELUS*, and *The Journal of Popular Culture.*

Julianne DiNenna is originally from Washington, D.C. Her poetry, essays, and short stories have been published in several journals including *Rattle*; *Journal of Compressed Creative Arts*; *Adanna Literary Journal; Gyroscope Review*; *Rise Up Review*; Stanford Medical School blog; *Months to Years*; *Italy, A Love Song*; *Susan B & Me*; *Offshoots*; *Grasslands Review*; and *Every Day Reading.* She blames her literary work on her frequent travels and on her Catholic upbringing.

Jillian Egan is a writer and voiceover artist originally from upstate New York who recently settled in North West England. Her latest project is a series of zines promoting working-class solidarity. More of her work can be found on Instagram: @mammarius.hex.

Leigh Eicke, PhD, is a writer and editor in Grand Rapids, Michigan. She is co-editor with Jeana DelRosso and Ana Kothe of *The Catholic Church and Unruly Women Writers: Critical Essays* (Palgrave MacMillan, 2007), *Unruly Catholic Women Writers: Creative Responses to Catholicism* (SUNY Press, 2013), and *Unruly Catholic*

Nuns: Sisters' Stories (SUNY Press, 2017). She works in adult literacy and serves as a lector and lay eucharistic minister in the Episcopal Church.

Becky Gould Gibson, PhD, taught English and women's studies at Guilford College until retiring in 2008. Her poems have appeared in journals and anthologies, including *Kalliope: A Journal of Women's Literature and Art*, *Iris: A Journal About Women*, *Feminist Studies*, *Adanna Literary Journal*, and *Adrienne Rich: A Tribute Anthology* (Split Oak Press, 2012). She has also published eight poetry collections, most notably *Need-Fire* (Bright Hill Press, 2007), *The Xanthippe Fragments* (St. Andrews University Press, 2016), and *Indelible* (The Broadkill River Press, 2018). These three books give voice to women whose words are missing from the historical record: Hild, Abbess of Whitby (615–680), Socrates' wife Xanthippe, and Lydia, "a seller of purple goods" mentioned in Acts 16. The poem printed here, "The Lydian Woman Speaks to the Dead Saint," is from her book *Indelible*.

Elizabeth Brulé Farrell used to write advertising copy in Chicago before moving to southeastern Massachusetts. Her poems have been published in *The Paterson Literary Review*, *Poetry East*, *The Perch*, *Just Like A Girl*, *Earth's Daughters*, *Pilgrimage*, *The Awakenings Review*, *The Healing Muse*, *Spillway*, *Watch My Rising*, *The Chaos of Angels*, *Desert Call*, and other publications. She has been a recipient of The Louise Bogan Memorial Award for Poetry. She is truly glad to have her poem be a part of this volume.

Lauren Frances Guerra, PhD, is visiting assistant professor in the Department of Theological Studies at Loyola Marymount University in Los Angeles, California. She is of Guatemalan-Ecuadorian descent and an active member of the Roman Catholic Church. She earned her doctorate in systematic and philosophical theology from the Graduate Theological Union, Berkeley. Her research interests include U.S. Latinx Theology, Theological Aesthetics, and Ethnic Studies. She approaches the theological task with the complexities of race, class, and gender in mind. Popular religion and community-based art inform her theologizing. Her long-term goal is to serve as an advocate for the U.S. Latinx community through her academic work.

Maryanne Hannan has published poetry in numerous religious and feminist journals and anthologies. She is the author of *Rocking Like It's All Intermezzo: 21st Century Psalm Responsorials* (Resource Publications, 2019). A cradle Catholic and a former Latin teacher, she lives in upstate New York.

Adrienne Keller, PhD, is a retired academic, happily living and writing in Charlottesville, Virginia. She is the author of *Psalms Turned Inward* and co-author of *Patterns of Relating: An Adult Attachment Perspective* as well as numerous academic articles, chapters, and presentations. Now she gratefully focuses on her nonacademic writing, much of which can be found on her blog, vabutsy.com.

Ana Kothe, PhD, is professor of comparative literature and humanities at the University of Puerto Rico, Mayagüez. Co-editor of three previous *Unruly* books with Jeana DelRosso and Leigh Eicke, she has published on several women writers from Sor Juana Inés de la Cruz in the seventeenth century to Carmen Boullosa in the twenty-first. Her research interests include women and religion, humor, and animals.

Devin E. Kuhn has a PhD in women's studies in religion from Claremont Graduate University. Her research investigates the intersections among theology, ethics, and popular culture. Her writing has appeared in *Religion Dispatches.* She lives with her partner and daughter on California's Central Coast, where they enjoy cycling, kayaking, and smashing the patriarchy.

Jennifer Hall Lee is a filmmaker and writer. She started her film career at Lucasfilm's Industrial Light & Magic; her credits include *Back to the Future II, Hook, Ghost, Beowulf,* and more. She is a documentary filmmaker, and her film *Feminist: Stories from Women's Liberation* is distributed by Women Make Movies. Her writing has appeared in books such as *Love Her, Love Her Not: The Hillary Paradox* (She Writes Press, 2015) and *Women's Rights: Reflections in Popular Culture* (ABC-Clio Greenwood, 2017), as well as in the *San Francisco Chronicle*, *Pasadena Star News*, and *ColoradoBoulevard.net*. She is a Pasadena Unified School District Trustee and lives in Altadena, California, with her husband and daughter.

Marci Madary, DMin, has ministered in the realm of spirituality throughout her professional life and is passionate about the intersection of theology and the lives of laity. Along with speaking at conferences and leading retreats, Marci is a facilitator, spiritual director, adjunct professor, and poet. She earned a Doctor of Ministry in spirituality at Catholic Theological Union; her thesis explores the dynamic of mutuality between women and men who minister together. Married and the mother of two young adults, she deeply treasures the relationships in her life.

Megan Merchant lives in the tall pines of Prescott, Arizona, with her husband and two children. She is the author of three full-length poetry collections—*Gravel Ghosts* (Glass Lyre Press, 2016), *The Dark's Humming* (2015 Lyrebird Award Winner, Glass Lyre Press, 2017), *Grief Flowers* (Glass Lyre Press, August 2018)—as well as four chapbooks and a children's book, *These Words I Shaped for You* (Philomel Books). She was awarded the 2016–17 COG Literary Award, judged by Juan Felipe Herrera; the 14thAnnual Beullah Rose Poetry Prize; and most recently, second place in the Pablo Neruda Prize for Poetry. She is an editor at *The Comstock Review*, and you can find her work at meganmerchant.wix.com/poet.

Dawn Morais, PhD, was born in Kerala, raised in Malaysia, and lives in Hawai'i. She teaches in the University of Hawai'i at Mānoa Honors Program. She advocates for marriage equality, environmental protection, a living wage, paid family leave, access to the ballot, tax fairness, and more. A product of a Franciscan schooling, she is a dissident Catholic who worships now at St. Elizabeth's Episcopal Church, which hosts the only Catholic Worker House in Hawai'i. Her work has been published in *Bamboo Ridge*, *Fugue*, *The Red*

Wheelbarrow, and *Merton Seasonal*. Her op-eds have appeared in the *Honolulu Star Advertiser*, *Civil Beat*, the *National Catholic Reporter*, *The Baltimore Sun*, and *HuffPost*. She had a career in IBM and led PR agencies in Malaysia and Honolulu. She is married to John Webster and has two adult children, Zubin and Sheela Jane Menon, and one grandson, all sent by the angels. She blogs at www.dawnmorais.com and guest blogs at https://feminismandreligion.com/. Her essay, "Political Engagement: A New Article of Lived Faith" just appeared in *The Value of Hawai'i 3: Hulihia, the Turning* (University of Hawai'i Press, 2020).

Jeannine Marie Pitas, PhD, is assistant professor of English and Spanish at the University of Dubuque in Iowa. She is the author of three poetry chapbooks, most recently *thank you for dreaming* (Lummox Press, 2018). Her first full-length collection of poetry, *Things Seen and Unseen*, was published by Mosaic Press in 2019. She is also a Spanish-English literary translator, and her translation of Uruguayan poet Marosa di Giorgio's *I Remember Nightfall* was shortlisted for the 2018 National Translation Award. She is the translation co-editor of *Presence: A Journal of Catholic Poetry*.

C. R. Resetarits has published poetry recently in *Yellow Medicine Review, North Dakota Quarterly, Modern Language Studies,* and *Native Voices: Indigenous American Poetry, Craft and Conversation* (Tupelo Press). Her poetry collection, *BROOD*, was published by Mongrel Empire Press in 2015. She lives in Faulkner-riddled Oxford, Mississippi.

Lizzie Sextro is a copywriter living in St. Louis, Missouri, with her partner, Caroline. She received her bachelor's degrees in theology and English from Loyola University Chicago and went on to receive her Masters of Theological Studies from the Boston College School of Theology and Ministry. Although she is no longer Catholic-identifying, she carries a deep appreciation for the history and ritual of the Church and for her nineteen years of Catholic education. Lizzie practices yoga in her free time and has made it her life's goal to read every work produced by her favorite unruly woman, Margaret Atwood. Her poem included here is inspired by another magnificent, unruly woman, Maya Angelou, author of the poem "Still I Rise" as well as numerous other groundbreaking works of poetry and prose. Lizzie would like to express her deep gratitude for all the unknown, unappreciated, unwelcomed, unruly women who came before her.

Celia Viggo Wexler is an award-winning journalist and nonfiction author. Wexler's first book, *Out of the News: Former Journalists Discuss a Profession in Crisis* (McFarland), won a national award for excellence from the Society of Professional Journalists. Her well-reviewed second book, *Catholic Women Confront Their Church: Stories of Hurt and Hope*, was published in September 2016 by Rowman & Littlefield. Her work has appeared in *The New York Times*, *The Washington Post*, the *San Francisco Chronicle*, *Columbia Journalism Review*, and *The Nation*. She graduated summa cum laude from the University of Toronto, where she earned the prestigious Governor-General's Medal in English Literature. She earned a graduate degree in journalism from Point Park University, Pittsburgh. She is mother to Valerie Wexler.

Valerie Wexler is an investigative and political researcher, writer, and organizer located in Washington, D.C. Her research has been cited or mentioned in numerous news outlets including Bloomberg, CNN, NBC, AP, *Politico*, *The Washington Post*, and *The New York Times*. A former Catholic feminist (now just a feminist), she is dedicated to working for social justice on both the local and national level. She is daughter to Celia Wexler.

Lindsey E. White is an aspiring writer, public interest attorney, and questioning Catholic. She is thrilled to contribute to *Unruly Catholic Feminists*, as it is one of her first appearances in print. She hopes to continue writing creatively from the Catholic part of herself in the future.

Sofia Zocca is a law student at Boston University School of Law. She holds a Bachelor of Arts in English and Sociology from Boston University, where she received departmental honors in English for her senior thesis, *Reclaiming the Garden: The Proto-feminist Poetry and Legacy of Aemilia Lanyer.* Her poems and short stories have appeared in BU's literary magazine, *Coup d'Etat*, and she is interested in Italian women's literature and British and American Gothic poetry.